AND IT WAS GOOD

Also by Madeleine L'Engle

Madeleine L'Engle

AND IT WAS GOOD

Reflections on Beginnings

Harold Shaw Publishers
Wheaton, Illinois

ISBN 0-87788-046-8

Printed in the United States of America

Library of Congress Cataloging in Publication Data

L'Engle, Madeleine.
  And it was good.

  (Wheaton literary series)
  1. Bible. O.T. Genesis I-XXI—Meditations.
2. God. 3. Christian life—1960-   . 4. L'Engle,
Madeleine.   I. Title.   II. Series.
BS1235.4.L46 1983   242'.5   83-8518
ISBN 0-87788-046-8

---

95 94 93 92 91 90 89   10 9 8 7 6 5 4

For
  Clyde and Martha Kilby
and
  Mel Lorentzen

CONTENTS

FOREWORD

MUCH OF THE BOOK of Genesis, particularly the early chapters with their unfolding of the creation narrative, is poetry. For years a persistent and hitherto unsolved question of mine has been, "Who was the poet of Genesis?" Was it the Lord God himself? Or Moses, the scribe of the Pentateuch? Or the scholars of the past and present who have involved themselves in translating the ancient Hebrew manuscripts into ringing contemporary language versions?

I think Madeleine L'Engle has given me an answer. In developing her concept of co-creativity and co-creators she helps me to see how it is possible for God and man to work together—the primal impulse of God as Maker, First Poet of the universe (*poet* means, literally, *maker*), inspiriting, ingodding human thinking and imagination until the divine word becomes enfleshed and is expressed in human language. In the rhythmical, idiosyncratic syllables and phrases of Scripture are expressed not only the infinite truth of God and his purposes, but the specificity, the particularity, the singularity of articulate human beings made in God's image. The creative process is thus seen complete in Genesis—the rich, cyclical cadences of "God said, 'let there be'... and it was so... and there was evening, and there was morning—one day" flows from action to story and poetry in a co-creating that is both genuinely divine and authentically human.

For the story of Genesis is my story. It is not simply a fragmented, legendary account seen dimly through the vast distance of eons. It is utterly concrete, believeable, actual, because it touches on things I myself touch—oceans, islands, fur, wings, leaves, fruit, as well as wonder, beauty, temptation, sacrifice, pain, disobedience, repentance, and restitution. The fresh joy of Adam and Eve in a verdant paradise is my own joy as I walk in the Illinois woods in spring. After grabbing clumsily at what looks good to me, and even infecting others with my greed, I feel both shame and alienation from God, and then I am Eve—ashamed, and afraid of the Creator who has been my closest friend, running with Adam from the Garden, from the fierce cherubim, ducking and cringing before the thrusting sword that turns and flashes with holy fire. Eve's travail in child-bearing is my own—I have undergone it five times—and her exultation in getting a child from the Lord has been multiplied in my own maternity.

I am not surprised at Madeleine's preoccupation with the glory of Eden, at her recognition of that which Jehovah declared *good* as it shines out in a million ways even from a creation flawed and broken by evil. Neither am I surprised at the satisfaction she finds in meditating on the diversity and beauty of the first creation—all freshly green, dew-soaked, fragrant, unpolluted. She and Hugh have their own Edenic spot at the foot of the pasture lands of Crosswicks, mossy, the light dappled with cool, leaf-shaped shadows even on the longest, hottest days of summer. This is Madeleine's *being* place, complete with brook and faithful dog, where, barefoot in the running water, she knows with all her senses the sharp delight of God's presence in creation. The reality of being herself made in God's image, a creator, rises in her there again and again, like sap in a tree every April. In the intimacy of this small, tree-lined, private place, Madeleine finds time to examine the microcosm; and from the spreading, glacial rocks that crown a neighbor mountain, or from the top deck of a freighter at the foot of the world she begins to penetrate the mysteries of the macrocosm. From such vantage points she finds a true perspective to bring to the most tragic or glorious or fleeting or ordinary of life's circumstances. Hers is the way of affirmation, not negation, yet she neither avoids nor evades pain, paradox, or mystery, but balances them with the confidence, often defined as faith, that God will fulfill his promises, will bring explanation and understanding in his own time.

As we worked together through the intricacies of the manuscript of *And It Was God*, time and time again I literally caught my breath at some of Madeleine's outrageous statements. "Madeleine, you *can't say* that!" I would explode, protesting the radical nature of her declarations—radical in the true sense of digging for and baring root principles. But reading further, penetrating deeper, I would grasp the holy logic of her conclusions and find myself acknowledging, "You not only *can* say that, you *should!*" In commanding such commitment and focused attention from her readers and drawing them down the avenues of her thinking she seems to be echoing the stringent demands of the God who "asks us to listen even when what he asks of us seems most outrageous."

Perhaps Madeleine's most valuable insights surface as

she reflects on the character of God, as Maker, Father—
sometimes implacable, never impassible—a stern Task-
master, and a loving Provider who is with us in our suffering
and shares in all our joy. It is he who undergirds Madeleine
in her creating. It is he who is seen on every page of this
book. And it is good.

Luci Shaw

Beginnings

1

A SMALL SHIP—a freighter—on a very large sea.

A cloudless blue sky, and the sun lighting an ocean which changed from blue to purple to steel grey as the wind rose and the waves lifted their crests.

We were caught in an unusual nautical event, a fair weather storm.

The crew strung ropes along all the walkways which did not already have rails. In the dining room the tablecloths were soaked with water to keep the dishes from sliding. People who travel on freighters are likely to be good sailors, so most of us made it in to dinner.

During the night we felt the wind continue to rise. We had to hold on to the sides of our bunks to keep from being thrown out, and sleep was out of the question. That morning it just happened that we had been given a sheet of paper explaining the Beaufort scale, which measures the severity of storms on a ratio of one to twelve. Where on that scale were we? As the wind rose, and the waves, we felt more than mere curiosity about it.

Our ship, though heavily laden with cargo at both ends, was rather light in the middle where the cabins and the public rooms were situated. Neither my husband nor I spoke the thought aloud, but later we confessed we both had had visions of the ship breaking in two. It was not that we rolled or hawed. It felt as though the ship was crashing into stone as it hit one mountainous wave after another.

We had been at sea only about a week, rejoicing at first in balmy weather, where at home in Connecticut there was snow and ice. We were both beginning to relax after weeks of very heavy work schedules. And I had turned back to Genesis as well as John's gospel for my Scripture reading, using the Gideon Bible in our cabin.

Something about the wildness of the weather started those great verses moving strongly through my mind. I was not really frightened by the storm, but I was, to put it mildly, ill at ease and uncomfortable, and so I rested on the great story of the Beginning.

In the beginning God created the heaven and the earth. In the beginning was the Word, and the Word was with God, and the Word was God. And the earth was without form, and void; and darkness was upon the face of the deep. And the Spirit of God moved upon the face of the waters.

In the beginning was the Word, with God; and the Spirit was in the beginning. Always there are all three faces of our trinitarian God. Always. The past—before time and space. Always. Now—during quiet. During storm. And the word *always* also looks forward, beyond when time and space will end.

*The same Word was in the beginning with God. All
things were made by him, and without him was not anything made that was made.*

One is very aware of time in the middle of a storm. I kept
looking at our travel clock, faintly luminous at two o'clock in
the morning. But outside, not a glimmer of light. Only the
dark violence of wind and wave. How long would it go on?
How long could it go on?

It is difficult for us who were born in time, into time,
and whose mortality will die in time—to time, to understand that before that extraordinary beginning, that first act
of creativity, that first epiphany, when God took nothing and
made something, there was no time, no space. Everything
began at the same moment. In the beginning.

*And God said, Let there be light. And there was light.
And God saw the light, that it was good, and God divided the light from the darkness. And God called the
light day, and the darkness he called night. And the
evening and morning were the first day.*

There's something of the feeling of that first day on a ship,
especially a small ship. Caught up as most of us are in the
complexities of daily living, we forget that we are surrounded by the creative power of Love. Every once in a
while we need to step aside from the troubles and pleasures
of our lives, and take a fresh look, a time to feel, and listen to
our Source. Ever since my husband has been on the TV
series, "All My Children," and gets a real vacation, we have
done our stepping aside by boarding an ocean freighter. In
mid-February, whenever possible, we embark on a small
ship in a large sea. (Having been married for twenty-five
years before we had spent more than two nights away from

home together only heightens our delight in having a real holiday.)

The day before we sailed into that extraordinary fair-weather storm, as our freighter moved down the east coast of South America to what is called "the Bottom of the World," our captain spoke to us. "As we get near the Strait of Magellan," he said, "be sure to look at the horizon. You'll never see it so clearly. There are no towns or cities to pollute the atmosphere."

It was true. Down there, when we looked at the horizon we saw *air*, air as it was meant to be when it was made. We saw clearly the beautiful curve of the earth. And at night we saw the Southern Cross in an absolutely black sky. I was astounded and awed at its blackness. Pure. Clear. With the stars blazing from out of it. There was none of the pinkish tinge we are used to seeing around the horizon from the city lights; even if we are as much as a hundred miles from the city, those lights still stain the sky of the "civilized" world.

And so, even before we moved into the wildness of the unexpected storm, we had a feeling of Genesis. The day after the storm was over and the ropes were taken down and we were able to balance as we stood or walked without legs wide apart, my husband asked the captain where we had been on the Beaufort scale. He replied laconically, "Eleven."

I stood at the rail and looked at the sea, which felt smooth again, though there were still whitecaps breaking the surface, and kept on with my thoughts. The first day. The beginning of time. Time, which, like matter, was created in that first great shouting of joy, of making nothing into something; time, a part of nature, which, like space, like all creation, will have an end. (All created things die. Before the seed can grow, it must be planted in the earth, and so die to itself before it can become a tree. Or a wave. Or a flying fish.)

But in the beginning, when all things were first shown forth, the light and the dark danced together; in the fullness of their time they comprehended each other; they knew each other, and it was good. It was very good.

God created. God *made*.

Night and day—that first flashing rhythm which marked the birth of time. Water and land. Galaxies and suns and planets and moons, all moving in the joyous dance of creation. Matter and time making music together.

God made. Fish and sea animals and birds. Land and land animals, every kind of living creature, ants and auks and aardvarks. Dromedaries and dragons and dinosaurs.

And God saw that it was good. And God said, let us make man in our image.

Our image, said the Trinitarian Creator, the Maker.

"Our" image, as it is translated in the *King James Bible*, is more in harmony with the original than some of the newer translations which say "my" image, completely missing the point.

If Christ suddenly appeared in Bethlehem two thousand years ago, as a surprising number of people seem to believe, how can there be unity in Trinity? Yes, for all three persons were there, always, inseparable, whole and holy.

So God said, Let us make man in our image . . . male and female.

Both male and female go to make the image of God, not a singleton, not an independent entity. Not *one:* how could one be *our* image? *Our* image, said God, not my image. Our image, male and female.

That it takes both male and female to complete the

image of God is not a new thought for me, but neither is it a static one. My own thinking about the balance of love and tension between male and female changes with each encounter. As a woman, I deny my own free will if I blame men for the patriarchal society into which I was born. Males cannot take over unless females permit it. And in permitting it, we erode male wholeness as well as our own. And *our* image is an image of wholeness—what we are meant to be.

In the beginning of the space/time continuum, night and day (female and male, according to Greek thinking) understood each other, as we need to understand each other now, if, in this time, we are not to destroy time, and ourselves along with it. I, as a woman, need to understand not only the men I encounter in my life, but the masculine in myself, just as men must seek to understand not only the women they meet, but the feminine in themselves. This is perhaps easier for women than for men, for through the centuries women have often had to be both mother and father, when their husbands were at sea, or at war, or, in my case, when my actor husband had to be on the road for months at a time with a play. Women have been allowed to affirm the nurturing and the intuitive in themselves, whereas more often than not men have been forced by society to limit themselves to the rational, fact-finding-and-proving part of their personalities. Women must be very gentle with men as they, as well as women, seek to regain the lost wholeness for which they were destined.

It takes two to make the image of God, not necessarily a male and a female, though this is the most obvious example. It takes all aspects of ourselves to be part of that image. And "our" image is an image of community, community which was in trinity in the beginning, and which will be after the eschaton, the end of time, when night and day and all of us will know each other again in the coming of the kingdom.

In that first epiphany, when matter was formless and space was empty, God created. How marvellous that there should be something rather than nothing! How marvellous that there *is*, rather than that there is not.

God created, and it was joy: time, space, matter. There *is*, and we are part of that is-ness, part of that becoming. That is our calling: co-creation. Every single one of us, without exception, is called to co-create with God. No one is too unimportant to have a share in the making or unmaking of the final showing-forth. Everything that we do either draws the Kingdom of love closer, or pushes it further off. That is a fearful responsibility, but when God made "man in our image, male and female," responsibility went with it. Too often we want to let somebody else do it, the preacher, or the teacher, or the government agency. But if we are to continue to grow in God's image, then we have to accept the responsibility.

God's image! How much of God may be seen in me, may I see in others? Try as we may, we cannot hide it completely.

A young reader knowing of my love of new words, sent me a beautiful one: namasté: I salute the God within you.

The words which have taught me most richly come in logical progression: *ontology:* the word about being; *ousia:* the essence of being, that which is really real; *ananda* (also sent me as a gift by a reader): that joy in existence without which the universe will fall apart and collapse. And now: *namasté.*

If we accept that God is within each of us, then God will give us, within us, the courage to accept the responsibility of being co-creators.

We live in a world which has become too complex to unravel; there is nothing we can do about it, we little people who don't have big government posts or positions of importance. But I believe that the Kingdom is built on the little things that all of us do. I remember my grandmother was fond of reciting:

> *Little drops of water,*
> *Little grains of sand*
> *Make the mighty ocean*
> *And the pleasant land.*

A single drop can't make even a puddle, but together, all our little drops and God's planning can make not only a mighty ocean but a mighty difference. Alone, there's not much we can do, but when Peter healed a cripple it was made very clear that it was not by his own power, but by the power of Christ, the creating Word, that the healing was accomplished.

This power is available to all of us. Indeed, with everything we do, we either use or reject it, for we do nothing in isolation. As the physicists who study the microcosm are discovering, *nothing* happens in isolation; nothing *exists* in isolation. Quanta, the tiny subatomic particles being studied in quantum mechanics, cannot exist alone; there cannot be *a* quantum, for quanta exist only in relationship to each other. And they can never be studied objectively, because even to observe them is to change them. And, like the stars, they appear to be able to communicate with each other without sound or speech;

> *there is neither speech nor language; but their voices are heard among them,*

sings the psalmist.

Surely what is true of quanta is true of the creation; it is true of quarks, it is true of human beings. We do not exist in isolation. We are part of a vast web of relationships and interrelationships which sing themselves in the ancient harmonies. Nor can we be studied objectively, because to look at us is to change us. And for us to look at anything is to change not only what we are looking at, but ourselves, too.

And our deepest messages of love are often conveyed without words. In my writing I have used the word *kything*, found in an old Scottish dictionary of my grandfather's, to express this communication without words, where there is "neither speech nor language." To kythe is to open yourself to someone. It is, for me, a form of intercessory prayer, for it is to be utterly vulnerable.

To some people it smacks of ESP. They are wary of such things, not being able to understand them. Kything is indeed a kind of ESP, although it goes much further, for it takes a deep faith in the goodness of creation and the power of love to open oneself in love and hope and faith. So it came as a shock to me when I received a letter asking me, with great sincerity, if kything was satanic. Evidently, to the writer, any form of extrasensory perception was of the devil. Of course, wherever there is good, in comes the devil at a gallop. But to kythe, to be with someone in that deepest communication which is beyond words, is of God, not of the devil. When I was a child, my test for real friendship was the test of silence: could I and my friend be together without speaking and be comfortable with each other? If the answer was Yes, then I could trust the friendship.

We do not love each other without changing each other. We do not observe the world around us without in some way changing it, and being changed ourselves. To listen to the news on radio or television is to be part of what is going on, and to be modified by it. But how on earth—or heaven— can that be reciprocal? *We* are changed by war and rumour of war, but how can we in turn change what changes us?

There are some obvious, small ways. We can join, if we are female, the League of Women voters. We can do volunteer work (despite a nine-to-five job) in the hospice movement. We can write our senators and congressmen. In the Greek play *Lysistrata* the women were so outraged by war that they banded together against the men to stop it. We are not as helpless as we may seem.

Those are a few of the obviously active ways. But there are less obvious ones that are equally important. I was asked how we could pray for our planet, with the devastating wars which are tearing it apart, with greed fouling the air we breathe and the water we drink. And I replied that the only way I know how to pray for the body of our planet is to see it as God meant it to be, to see the sky as we sometimes see it in the country in wintertime, crisp with stars, or to see the land with spring moving across it, the fruit trees flowering and the grass greening, and at night hearing the peepers calling back and forth, and the high, sweet singing of the bats.

In the spring, the early spring, during the height of the Falkland crisis, I knelt on the damp earth planting onion sets, and smelling the rich growing odour of the freshly turned garden, and the pungency of the onions. Planting onions that spring was an act of faith in the future, for I was very fearful for our planet. It has long seemed likely that if there is atomic devastation, it will not come from one of the great powers. (Russia does not want war any more than we do. The land of Russia is still not healed from the terrible wounds of World War II. The scars are still visible. Nor is China hungry for war.) If we blunder into the folly of atomic warfare it is more likely to come from something seemingly as absurd as the battle over the inhospitable Falklands than from something predictable.

So I planted onions, and hoped, and prayed, and suddenly I was aware of being surrounded by the song of the birds, making an ecstasy of melody, and their joy was a strengthening of hope. As I sat back on my heels, the better to listen, the birdsong was an affirmation of ultimate all-rightness and also of immediate all-rightness, despite the news to which we were anxiously listening. The birds know. We sophisticated people have forgotten what the "primitive" people have always known, that the birds *know,* and that a change in their song is a portent of change to come, usually terrible change. But this singing of the birds was their own spring song, which I have heard year after year, and so my heavy heart lifted.

That evening Hugh and I saw something we had never seen before, two robins in a mating dance, and that, too, was affirmation. It may seem that the beauty of two robins can do little to heal the horrors of our planet, but I believe that in their dance they were not only following the call of spring, but healing—or helping to heal—all that has gone wrong with the sweet green earth on which they live.

A year ago a family of robins made their nest in our garage. We are used to having barn swallows come in and try to set up light housekeeping, but not robins. However, one day we noticed that on the back of a bicycle which hangs on the wall was a robin's nest. By standing on a box, we could see the eggs, naturally a beautiful robin's-egg blue! And of course we could not use the garage until the eggs were hatched and the fledglings had learned to fly. That was the spring that the gypsy moths devastated the land, de-foliating a tree in an hour. Mountainsides were as bare and brown as in winter. And it was our son's theory that this particular robin family had "known" that the trees were going to lose their protecting leaves, and so they had come into the garage, contrary to pattern, to keep their babies safe.

This spring the robins were back in the newly-dressed trees in their re-created green, and in our area of the countryside the gypsy moths have done little damage.

———◆◆———

The Falkland crisis ended, but the fear of war does not. With each onslaught of terror it hits us anew. Why do we tend to forget that this has been a century of fear, when the second half of the century has been gripped in the fear of atomic horror?

A reminder of how long this fear has been with us came to me when I turned to some old journals to type out for my children the stories of their births, and some of the things they did and said when they were little. I don't go back to those journals very often, and I was surprised at the many entries which showed my anguish about the possibility of atomic warfare.

One time in the fifties when we were listening in anxiety to every radio newscast, trying not to let our small children see how anxious we were, I recorded putting them to bed. Our youngest was four. His prayers were dictatorial to God (as only a four-year-old can be dictatorial), and intimate. That night, in the middle of his long "God blesses," he said, "God, please don't let there be any more wars. Please just let everybody die of old age." And, a few months later: "... and God, please remember about do unto others as you would they do to you. Please make them *do* these words. Make them think. Make them think, and not destroy this world."

So we all continue to pray for the planet, visualizing the pussy willows turning furry in the spring, listening to the songs of the insects and tree toads in the autumn, hearing the rain fall on the thirsty gardens, seeing the unique blue of the robins' eggs.

The robins affirm, for me, the validity and vitality of creation. The robin's song is as important to the heavenly harmonies as is the turning of the galaxies. And it is all, all held in the love of God.

One of the early words by which the ancient Hebrews knew God was El. El—the Lord. Beth-el, for instance, means the house of God. So I find it helpful, wherever and whenever possible, to call God El, or el, rather than using the masculine or feminine pronoun, because the name *el* lifts the Creator beyond all our sexisms and chauvinisms and anthropomorphisms.

We human creatures, made in the image of God, in church as well as out, too often reject instead of affirming the Word which has proven to be the cornerstone. And we worry, too often, about peripheral things. (Like baptism: is dunking more valid than sprinkling?) And we are continuing to worry about sexist words to the point where we are coming close to destroying language. To call God either him or her, he or she, is in both cases to miss the wholeness of the Creator. And so we lose all sense of proportion, and try to clamp God once again within our own broken image.

And so I return to the reality of our trinitarian God of creation, el.

El. That power of love. That holy thing. Do we believe that it was a power of love which created everything and saw it was good? Is creation purposeful? Or is it some kind of cosmic accident? Do our fragments of lives have meaning? Or are we poor human beings no more than a skin disease on the face of an unfortunate planet? Can we see the pattern and beauty which is an affirmation of the value of all creation?

On the cover of the May, 1982 *Scientific American* is a beautiful photograph of a "pattern of radio emission from the gigantic elliptical galaxy IC 4296. (There are so many quadrillions of galaxies that the scientists, alas, have run out of names and resorted to numbers. I am grateful for the psalmist's affirmation that God knows *all* the stars by name.) The galaxy, probably a member of the Centaurus cluster of galaxies, is 120 million light years away. It is nonetheless the closest of the 'classical' radio sources: the sources consisting of two symmetrical lobes of radio emission... the patch is really two jets of ionized gas emerging in opposite directions from the center of the galaxy... The distance between the lobes is almost a million light years."

The macrocosm. Too enormous for our finite minds readily to comprehend.

And then the microcosm. The distances between the parts of an electron are proportionately as vast as the distance between those lobes of radio emission from a galaxy.

What does that do to our concept of size? It either makes us throw up our hands in horror at the over-awesome incomprehensibility of creation, or it makes us cry out in joy at the total unimportance of size, for all, all of it is held in God's loving hand. "See, I will not forget you," el assures us in the book of the prophet Isaiah. "I have carved you on the palm of my hand."

———◆◆———

I am grateful for our freighter vacations which provide stress release from the normal strains of daily living. But though there are no phone calls, no interruptions, nothing that *has* to be done, even a vacation on a freighter does not offer a safe and placid world. Creation is still wildly beautiful, and it is still wild. Eleven is mighty close to twelve on the Beaufort scale, and twelve is disaster.

If I affirm that the universe was created by a power of love, and that all creation is good, I am not proclaiming safety. Safety was never part of the promise. Creativity, yes; safety, no. All creativity is dangerous. Even with the advances of science, women still die in childbirth. Babies are born with distorted limbs or minds. To write a story or paint a picture is to risk failure. To love someone is to risk that you may not be loved in return, or that the love will die. But love is worth that risk, and so is birth, its fulfillment.

This is no time for a child to be born,
With the earth betrayed by war & hate
And a nova lighting the sky to warn
That time runs out & the sun burns late,

That was no time for a child to be born,
In a land in the crushing grip of Rome;
Honour & truth were trampled by scorn—
Yet here did the Saviour make his home.

When is the time for love to be born?
The inn is full on the planet earth,
And by greed & pride the sky is torn—
Yet Love still takes the risk of birth.

Anyone embracing Christianity for the sake of safety is going to distort the broken body even further. The desire for safety at any expense ultimately leads to death. It is the desire for safety which has made some people take refuge in religions which provide all the answers, make their members feel more saved than people who don't belong to their group, and promise freedom from danger. Insistence on static answers has brought about the recurring conflicts between science and religion.

At a writers' conference I was asked by a young man, "Do you believe in evolution?"

I had been talking about structure in fiction, not about

science, and the question was asked in the sort of belligerent manner that told me he was waiting to pounce on any answer, no matter what, as "wrong."

A crowded lecture room during a lecture on techniques of fiction was neither the time nor the place to get into an argument about evolutionism versus creationism, and in any event I find little to argue about. So I replied that I thought that God could create in any way which seemed good to el.

And that, indeed, is what I think. The only reason I can find for all the shouting about *how* God created is that it allows some people to stop thinking, to settle back into the safety of their rut, to stop thinking about what it is really all about.

What it is really about is that creation is God's. It is el who has made us, and not we ourselves. To argue about *how* God made us is to argue about non-essentials. As far as I am concerned, it doesn't matter a whit how God created. The important thing is that creation is God's, and that we are part of it, and being part of creation is for us to be co-creators with el in the continuing joy of new creation.

That is a great calling, and when we argue about *how* God created us, we forget our vocation, and the tempter rejoices. I'm all for genuine scientific research, but when we argue about *how*, rather than *if*, or *why*, we miss the point. In a world where fewer and fewer people believe in God at all, where life is for so many an unimportant accident with no meaning, where we are born only to slip back into annihilation, we need to stop arguing and affirm the goodness of creation, and the power of love which holds us all.

——◆◆——

As far as the evidence of science shows today (and the evidence of science is always open to change with new discoveries), evolution seems a likely explanation of how all the galaxies, solar systems, planets, creatures, human beings came to be. There are holes in this theory, things left out, things left unresolved, but that we "thinking reeds" have evolved slowly, the original unicellular creature becoming ever more and more complex, until brains were developed which were complex enough to ask questions, seems consistent with present knowledge. One of the still open questions in the debate is the extraordinarily rapid development of the brain pan from something tiny to the much larger one which contains and protects our complex brains. Why this development came about more swiftly than the ordinarily slow process would account for is one of the still unexplained mysteries. But the rapid development of the cranium and the cranial cavity happened, and with our complex brains we think, and we ask questions, and often we want them answered before we have gathered enough evidence.

If new evidence should prove that evolution is not how it all happened, that won't do anything to change the nature of God, any more than Galileo's discoveries changed the nature of God. Nor would it shatter my faith. The Lord of Creation makes as el chooses, and only el knows how. "I will be what I will be," God replied to Moses when asked about his name. The options are all open, free. Free of all the restrictions we human beings try to impose on our Maker. Free to offer us an example of freedom which we hardly dare contemplate.

Creation continues lavishly, and we are part of it. Not only are stars and people and fireflies born, not only do they die, but what we as creatures do during our lifespan makes a difference. We are not just passive, acted upon; we are also actors in the great drama of creation. As to the passionate arguers about creationism versus evolutionism, I still think they're missing the point. The more hotly they argue, the more widely do they miss the point. The more zealous they grow in defending their cause (like the church establishment of Galileo's day) the less are they able to sit back calmly and observe the evidence and say, "This, too, is the Lord's."

When I am most defensive about something, arguing hotly that I am right, it is time for me to step back and examine whatever it is I am trying to prove. When I am refusing to listen to anyone else, intractably defending some position or other (like doctors refusing Semilweisse's radical suggestion that they wash their hands before touching open wounds) then I am incapable of being a co-creator with God. God urges us to be willing to change, to go out into the wilderness, to wrestle with angels, to take off our shoes when we step on holy ground.

And to listen. God asks us to listen, even when what el asks of us seems most outrageous.

——◆◆◆——

It has long struck me with joy and awe that the theory of evolution is not contrary to the teaching of the Bible. One of the many extraordinary things about those first passages in Genesis is that they so nearly describe what has come to be recognized as the order of evolution. What matter if, in the language of great poetry, a few billennia are the first day, and a few more the second?

The amazing thing is that at the beginning there was darkness, formless and empty, and the Spirit brooding, brooding almost as though getting ready to hatch creation, and then the Word shouting for joy, and here we are! The Word spoke, and from nothing came the glory and music and pattern of a universe.

And how long, in cosmic time, were the billenia which made up each of the days of creation?

Hugh and I lay on the top deck of our little ship at night and looked at the stars, the nearest one in that hemisphere perhaps seven light years away, and the next one seventy, and others seven hundred, seven thousand, seven million. We were looking not at a one-dimensional sky, but a four-dimensional one, a multi-dimensional one, seeing out to the furthest reaches of space and time as we lay on one small spot on the top deck of a freighter; and that small spot in the space/time continuum was moving at approximately ten knots an hour. The planet, too, was moving, as it turned daily on its axis and yearly in its journey around the sun. And the sun was moving in the great turning of the galaxy, our Milky Way. In that magnificent immensity we realized, suddenly, how limited our view of time usually is.

We were looking at the brilliantly lit sky not only in our own present, but in the long past of most of the stars. Perhaps one of those sparkling diamonds was no longer there; we were seeing it so many million light years ago; perhaps it had gone out long before there was human life on this planet, and we were just now seeing its fire. How much time we were seeing, as well as space!

On a small ship the ability to be aware of our tiny, yet significant part in the interdependence of all of God's creation returns, and one's mind naturally turns to cosmic questions, rather than answers. Seeing the glory of the unpolluted horizon, the brilliance of the Southern Cross against the black velvet sky, opened up questions about creation and the Creator.

And laughter, too, for though we cannot take ourselves seriously enough, we can also take ourselves far too seriously.

One of the sailors remarked casually as he was swabbing down the deck, "It's a short walk from the womb to the tomb," and jolted us back from cosmic time to mortal time.

But mortal time is part of cosmic time, and during that short walk we are given glimpses of eternity, eternity which was before time began, and will be after time ends. The

Word, who moved into time for us and lived with us, lives, as Christ, in eternity; so, when we live in Christ, when Christ lives in us we, too, are free from time and alive in eternity.

On the ship we moved from time zone to time zone, resetting our clocks, a reminder that our time follows the movement of the planet. And within one time zone there are probably a million different perceptions of time.

Every summer we watch eagerly for the hummingbirds to come sip the nectar of delphinium and bee balm outside our kitchen windows. They hover by the flowers, seeming to achieve a stillness in the air, their wings moving so rapidly that we cannot see the motion. I have been told that their perception of time is so much faster than ours that to the tiny birds we human beings, moving at fewer rpm (or mph) do not even appear to be moving. So, according to our human perception of time a century may seem long, but all that has happened since that first moment of creation is no more than the flicker of God's eye. In the life-span of a star, an ordinary star like our sun, our lives are such a fragment of a fragment as to seem practically non-existent, even if we live four score years and ten, like my mother, or even five score, like my grandfather. So, according to one perception of time, the zealous creationists are right—God created everything in an instant—or, rather, seven days; and according to another perception of time, the pragmatic evolutionists are right, and life has evolved slowly over our chronological millennia. And, according to *any* perception of time, we human creatures with our brief, mortal lives are nevertheless so important to the Creator that el came to live with us; we are so beloved!

Since we live in time, it is almost impossible for us to understand that eternity is not a time concept, that it has nothing to do with the passage of time. The astrophysicist's concept of time has changed radically in the past half century. Time is not, as the old hymn suggests, a never-ending stream. Time, like the rest of us creatures, is complex and paradoxical and full of quirks and surprises.

Sandol Stoddard in *The Hospice Movement,* quotes Dr. Cicely Saunders: "We learn, for example, that time has no fixed meaning as such. An hour at the dentist seems like forever, but an hour with someone you love flies past. And yet, wait a little and look back on it. The hour of discomfort and anxiety is totally forgotten. What we remember forever is the hour of love."

The hour of love is the hour when God's creature, time, and el's human creatures, like us, collaborate with each other.

In New York, where we must live most of the year, we are aware of time largely because we are too busy; we have too many appointments. Like the White Rabbit we constantly cry out in distress, "I shall be late!" But in the days before time-pieces, when the rhythm of the seasons was essential to survival (as it was to the ancient nomadic Hebrews, to Abraham and Sarah) people were far more conscious of time than we are. Right timing was an integral part of prayer and of life. If the crops were not planted and harvested at the right time, there would not be enough to eat. Understanding the rhythms of nature was literally essential to survival, physically and psychically, and there was not the brokenness between the two that has come about in our time.

Scripture is constantly breaking through chronos into kairos. All those hundreds of years before the birth of Jesus, Job cried out of the intensity of his pain and grief an incredible affirmation:

I know that my Redeemer lives, and that he shall stand at the last day on earth, and though worms destroy this body, yet in my flesh shall I see God, whom I shall see for myself, and whom my own eyes shall behold, though my reins be consumed within me.

For at that last day we shall truly understand the meaning of creation and the story of Genesis. We shall truly understand what it means to be co-creators with the Lord of creation. God's time is always *now,* and in this eternal *now* our Redeemer lives, and we shall see him, face to face.

Calling God Abba, *Daddy*

2

ONE DAY SHORTLY after we'd crossed the equator, heading
north, we saw a pod of what the captain guessed was between one and two *thousand* dolphins sporting about our
little ship. There before our eyes was the joy of creation. It
was all Hugh could do to keep me from climbing the rail and
diving overboard to join their joy. Our joy. Our leaping and
diving and pirouetting. Our ocean. Our sky. Our joy in our
Creator.

The anonymous author of *The Cloud of Unknowing*
writes: "There are helps which the apprentice in contemplation should employ, namely, lesson, meditation, and orison,
or, as they are most generally called, reading, thinking, and
praying."

Good advice, which I try to heed during my daily times
with the Bible, so that sometimes after only a few verses my
mind will move into "free fall" and sometimes the thoughts

stray far from the words I have just read, and yet lead me into prayer. On a ship, time stretches beyond the boundaries of chronology, into real time, kairos, where it is possible to read more slowly, think more deeply, and pray more naturally, than during the usual over-scheduled days of chronos.

But something else, even beyond those excellent words of help for Scripture reading, made me go back to book 1, chapter 1, verse 1, of the Gideon Bible. That was the Lenten lections I was reading morning and evening, and which made me ask anew:

Who is this el, this Creator? Who was it to whom Jesus was always referring, and to whom he was always faithful? Who was it to whom Jesus prayed?

There are so many preconceptions encrusting our idea of the Father to whom Jesus turned in prayer, in joy, in anguish, that it is almost impossible to remove all the barnacles of tradition and prejudice which have accumulated over the years, and see and hear el freshly.

Each time I come to the story of Jesus' baptism it hits me with renewed force. After his baptism, during which the Holy Spirit descended upon him, that same Holy Spirit led Jesus into the wilderness to be tempted. That never ceases to shock me. It was not an evil spirit who led Jesus into the wilderness. It was not a fallen angel. It was the Holy Spirit. And this story is as crucial to the New Testament as the Exodus is to the Old.

Jesus insisted that his cousin, John, baptize him. And though John proclaimed that he was merely the forerunner of one whose sandal strap he was unworthy to unloose, he did as Jesus asked. And as Jesus came up out of the water, he saw the heavens opening, and the Spirit, like a dove, descending upon him. And there came a voice from heaven saying,

"You are my beloved Son, in whom I am well pleased."

Whom do we pray to? If we are to pray, we must know where our prayers are directed. Jesus prayed to his Father. And here again we have, in this century, a source of confusion. It was my good fortune to have a father I could respect and honour as well as love. But there are many people who are not granted this blessing, who have fathers who are domineering, or weaklings, or incestuous, or alcoholics, or sadists, or anything but models of a true father. Jesus called the Master of the Universe *Abba;* daddy. Jesus' earthly father, Joseph, was a man he could admire, a man with enough sense of his own self to be able to accept Mary for his wife under the most unusual of circumstances. But what about the rest of us, living in this time of extreme sexual confusion? There was plenty of sexual confusion in Jesus' world, too, especially in the Roman culture where license and perversion were the order of the day. Nevertheless Jesus constantly referred to his heavenly Father, and he taught us to pray: Our Father.

Praying to the Father is easy for me, since my image of a father is of someone with total integrity. Not that my father was perfect—anything but. He had a volatile temper—which I have inherited. He had wildly fluctuating moods. Before he died (I was seventeen) he often made me angry and now I understand him better than I did then. But he never gave an answer to a question to which he had no answer. If he promised me anything, I knew that I could trust that promise, and it gave me a sense of the meaning of promises which helps me to this day.

Jesus calls the Creator *Father,* and for him it is a valid image. For those of us who are only confused or hurt by this image it is not as easy. Perhaps it helps to remember that it is an image, and an image is only a way of groping toward the real. Yet some of us may find in the image of the Father the parent that we always longed for, and needed, the parent that our human father never was. We have to look at, and take seriously, Jesus' image, whether or not it is one which is creative for us. What is it that we trust most? Is it the turning of the stars in the heavens? That, for me, is another image of the Creator. Julian of Norwich called Christ her sister. John of the Cross and John Donne used the powerful language of romantic love. Recently a young friend wrote to me about her reading the Bible in French. "I wanted to share with you one of my discoveries—it's one that Julian of Norwich would have liked. The other day I was reading the beginning of the Gospel of John. It goes,

> *Au commencement était la Parole, et la Parole était avec Dieu, et la Parole était Dieu. Elle était au commencement avec Dieu.*

" '*She* was with God from the beginning.' Although I think too much fuss is made regarding sexist language, it was a real treat to see Jesus—la Parole—spoken of in feminine terms."

It is Jesus of Nazareth, the Word as human being, who calls God *Abba*. It is the Word, willingly and lovingly limiting itself in the form of what, as Word, Word had created—a sacrifice far beyond our comprehension. But if the Word, as Jesus, could call out, "Abba!" so can I.

We all have our own images, and they nourish us, but ultimately the Lord to whom we pray is beyond all images, all imagining.

The Holy Spirit came upon Jesus in the form of a dove—another image—and then that same Holy Spirit led Jesus into the wilderness to be tempted. Why? Why tempt us? Why tempt Jesus?

It was at the moment of his baptism that Jesus was

recognized as Messiah, the Promised One. If, as Jesus, he was fully man as well as fully God, there had to come a time of recognition of his vocation. And a vocation must be tested. That is why, in a monastery or convent, there is a period of postulancy, of novitiate. Is this vocation real? Its reality must be tested.

So Jesus fasted. And he prayed. And at the end of his long period of fasting, when he was weak with hunger, the tempter attacked. "If you're really the Son of God," he urged, "turn these stones into bread."

And Jesus wouldn't. He could have, but he wouldn't. He simply quoted from Deuteronomy:

"Man shall not live by bread alone, but by every word of God."

Then the devil took him to Jerusalem and set him on the highest pinnacle of the temple and suggested that he jump off, just to prove that he really was the Son of God. And the devil, being very clever, and knowing Scripture better than most of us, quoted the Psalms:

"He shall give his angels charge over you, to keep you, and in their hands they will bear you up, lest you dash your foot against a stone."

And Jesus knew that if he jumped the angels would hold him up and he would not be hurt. And since he knew Scripture even better than Satan he quoted Deuteronomy right back:

"It is written: you shall not tempt the Lord your God."

But Satan, still hopeful, took him to a high mountain, and because Satan was an angel, even if a fallen one, he still had great power and used it to show Jesus all the kingdoms of the earth in a moment of time. And he said, "I can give you all this." And he could. And Jesus knew that he could, for Satan is the prince of this world, and in the world he has proven far too often how powerful he is. He said to Jesus, "I can give you all this, and all the world's glory, without any suffering on your part, for it is mine to give."

And it was. And it is.

But Jesus said,

"Get away from me, Satan."

and again he quoted:

"You shall worship the Lord your God, and him only shall you serve."

And the devil left him, and angels came and ministered to him.

One by one Jesus turned down the world's great temptations. Satan still uses those three; he doesn't need any others; we still fall for the same ones, over and over again. When we pray,

"Lead us not into temptation."

we are asking the Holy Spirit not to test us as Jesus was tested, for we have seen that we are not immune to all that Satan offers us, as individuals, as churches, as the establishments of science and medicine and education and any other human establishment we can think of. We fall into one or another of the temptations, often deluded into thinking that what we are doing is for the best. We want short cuts to the Kingdom. We want it to be easy. We want to be pleased with ourselves—which is very different from loving ourselves. And so we heed the temptations. But Jesus didn't, because his whole being was rooted in his Father, the God who created heaven and earth and saw that it was all good.

It is impossible to understand the New Testament without a firm grounding in the Old. Jesus quoted again and again from Hebrew Scripture (and not just when he was getting rid of the devil). The writers of the Gospels assumed that those who heard them would be familiar with Hebrew Scripture. The quotations are not credited or cross referenced because as a part of daily prayer they were a familiar part of living. The God of the Old Testament is the God in and with and through whom Jesus lived, the God he refused to tempt, the God he served, even unto death.

I tend to stray from that God. All my false preconceptions get in my way, and these preconceptions surely please Satan, for they turn me from the Creator to the tempter who is much more "reasonable" and who, *in worldly terms*, has more power. Power is what Satan offers us, whereas God keeps pointing out that we serve el best in our weakness, so that we can acknowledge that it is the Creator choosing to work through us, his fragile creatures. It is God who has made us, and not we ourselves. But because we enjoy feeling powerful, we accept Satan's offers.

And look what happens. Just turn around. Watch the news on TV. Read the daily papers. Walk along a city street.

And so as I turned to Genesis, chapter 1, verse 1, I tried to read without all the preconceptions which have been built up over the centuries—a task I understood was not completely possible, but which could nevertheless be attempted. And at sea it was made easy, for the ocean and the sky were there to help and to encourage. And to pray for me.

I stood at the rail looking down at the ocean and saw the foil-like flickering of flying fish, and it struck me that knowledge is always open to change; knowledge, not wisdom. If it is not open to change it is not knowledge, it is prejudice.

———◆◆———

One day in very early spring I spent several hours autographing and answering questions at a delightful bookshop in a college town. In the late afternoon a young man who had been standing around, listening, came up to me and said, "I've really enjoyed what you've been saying to people, but I haven't read any of your books because I hear they're very religious."

At that, all my little red flags of warning unfurled and began flapping in the wind. "What do you mean by religion?" I asked. "Please define it. Hitler was very religious. Khoumeini is very religious. The communists are very religious. What do you mean by religion?" And then with astonishment I heard myself saying, "My religion is subject to change without notice."

And I felt that I had received a profound revelation.

As God has revealed elself throughout history, our concept of the Creator has changed and deepened. If we close ourselves off to revelation we are, in a real way, silencing God. If God is *I will be what I will be*, (which is what el replied when Moses asked "Who are you?") then our understanding of el's ways has to be open, too. A few years ago a popular lapel button read, *Please be patient with me, God isn't finished with me yet.* Did we really understand what that button was saying? If I discover that my concept of God is becoming limited, then I am beginning to shut myself off from revelation. And if I assume that my concept of God is final, I have fallen for Satan's temptations, because if I decide that my concept of God is final, then I am falling into hubris.

Faith and religion are not the same thing. Although my

42

faith may falter, it has to do with the constancy of God's love. Religion, which is the expression of faith, may find different expressions appropriate in different times and places and to different people, and the variety of these expressions can enlarge our perceptions and deepen our faith.

John Wesley Watts, who lived in West Virginia in the nineteenth century, wrote his own epitaph as he lay dying, and subsequently it was engraved on his tomb: *John Wesley Watts: A Firm Believer in Jesus Christ, Jeffersonian Democracy, and the Methodist Episcopal Church.*

I respect his conviction, but it is conviction, not faith. I come closer to defining and describing faith when I remember the great preacher Phillips Brooks, who was asked by an earnest questioner why he was a Christian. He thought seriously for a moment, then replied, "I think I am a Christian because of my aunt, who lives in Teaneck, New Jersey."

Or, as my friend Canon Tallis puts it, "A Christian is someone who knows one."

If I have faith, it is because I have met faith, I have seen it in action. And this faith is never a vague, pie-in-the-sky kind of thing. Heaven is not good because life is bad; the quality of our lives while we live them is preparation for heaven.

Protecting
God

3

IN THE BEGINNING God looked at creation and called it good. Very good.

There was nothing, and then came the mighty acts of creation, darkness and light, sea and land, fish and birds and beasts and finally man—man made in the image of God, male and female.

And of course as soon as this glorious creature appeared on the scene, along came confusion and conflict. And story.

No matter what else can be said about human beings, we do provide good stories. One of my favorite Hassidic tales ends, "God made man because he loves stories." And story is where we have learned to look for truth.

Time is God's. We are God's. Creation is God's. Yet even as we attempt to regulate our dogmas in the church we adopt a proprietary attitude. In fact, we tend to try to protect God. For example, we explain exactly how el created everything, as though we knew better than el how the

Creator chose to create. When we try to protect God, all we do is to stop our understanding of God from growing and deepening, because if we are open to new discoveries in the world within or without, it might change our comfortable image of God. In a fairly recent issue of *Christianity Today,* a magazine for which I have deep respect, the entire issue was taken up with issues of creationism, with theologians and scientists trying to explain, without doubt, exactly how God started it all. Though the magazine tried to be fair, to publish more than one point of view, the whole thing left me exhausted and frustrated. Some of the articles were so defensive about exactly how it all happened, that I found them difficult to read. I am not comfortable in a closed system where there are no questions left to ask, or where questions are shunned as heresy.

In *The Meaning of Persons* Dr. Paul Tournier points out that scientists are a great deal more humble now than they were half a century ago. It is a pity that more theologians do not also have this humility before God's mighty acts of creation.

Why do people who are Christian feel so zealously that they have to protect God from truth? How can a scientific discovery, no matter how radical, be upsetting to a Creator who made all things, who is all Truth? God never promised us that truth would be easy, but he never warned us to shun it; he urged us to seek it, in order to be free. Often when we wrestle with truth we are reflecting Jacob's night of wrestling with the angel.

Simone Weil writes, "For it seemed to me certain, and I still think so today, that one can never wrestle enough with God if one does so out of pure regard for truth. Christ likes us to prefer truth to him because, before being Christ, he is truth. If one turns aside from him to go towards the truth, one will not go far before falling into his arms."

But we keep on trying to protect God, in order to keep him in our own little corner. When our eldest child was baptized in the Episcopal Church, my beloved Mrs. O' defied her Roman Catholic Church in order to go to the baptism.

Now things have changed so that when I am at Mundelein College I stay in the convent with the sisters and go to Mass with them in the morning, and that is great joy.

Only a decade or so ago in the Episcopal Church my Southern Baptist husband was—at least in a good many churches—not welcome. And I would not, could not, go to a Lord's Table which excluded Hugh. Why did we ever fear that God could not protect his own table? He is the Host— why did we feel that we had to check over the guest list for him?

That, too, has changed. Our religion is not closed from revelation; we are beginning to trust creation to the Creator, and to understand that our own awareness of the *hows* of creation truly must be subject to change without notice. But we cannot have this openness unless our faith in God as Lord of all is bedrock under our feet.

How we need this rock!

Paul, in his first letter to the Christians in Corinth, emphasizes the firmness of the rock, and the eternal *is*-ness of Christ, when he writes:

All our ancestors were under the cloud . . . and all passed through the sea; and were all baptized into Moses in the cloud and in the sea; and did all eat the same spiritual meat; and did all drink the same spiritual drink; for they drank of that spiritual Rock that followed them: and that Rock was Christ.

Christ with us always, before the journey, during it, after the end. That is the rock under our feet, the rock which

47

springs forth with healing, thirst-quenching water. The Trinity has always been a unity; the Father, who will be what el will be, the Holy Spirit, before creation, brooding over the universe. And then the Word shouting for joy.

And it was good. We have done much to distort and wound that good—that distortion and pain are results of the gift of free will. But that does not make the original good any less glorious.

And I turn to story, for enlightenment. Some of the stories Jesus tells about our places at the table say a good deal to me here.

Story is paramount throughout Scripture, beginning with the beginning. In the Book of Genesis alone is all the material for a flaming best seller—sex, incest, virtue, violence, greed, conflict, lust, love, murder—it's all there.

The first human characters in this amazing drama are Adam and Eve, who were expelled from Eden. In order to understand this story, we have to recognize that it is told only from the point of view of the fall of this planet, whereas this planet was falling for something which had already taken place in more cosmic terms.

There was war in Heaven.

That fact was part of the revelation to St. John the Divine.

Michael and his angels fought against the dragon, and the dragon fought, and his angels, and prevailed not; neither was their place found any more in heaven. And the great dragon was cast out, that old serpent, called the devil, and Satan, who deceives the whole world; he was cast out into the earth, and his angels were cast out with him.

And Satan and his angels are still here. When the Lord, in the beginning of the Book of Job, asks Satan what he has been doing, he answers that he has been walking up and down, to and fro over the earth. (Looking to see what he could do? He finds plenty to do, then and now. Alas.)

The war in heaven is still going on, and we are part of it. It is easy to see wickedness here on this planet, in every newscast, newspaper, magazine; a little less easy, perhaps, to perceive that it is not limited to our earth, or our solar system, or our galaxy.

As we think about this vast, cosmic battle, it is far too easy to fall into dualism, to think of darkness and light battling each other from the beginning, as some of the eastern religions proclaim. But if God created everything and saw that it was good, then something must have happened to this good, to change and distort it. The problem is not from without; it rose from within. And we have within each of us some of this wrongness, and too often we refuse to see it, and don't understand why we are not happy, nor why our faith seems a dim thing, nor why our prayers are like dead ashes.

But what is faith? We all know people who are convinced of the rightness of their faith, and yet seem to be narrowminded and sometimes downright vicious. People who are convinced of the rightness of their religion are quite literally burning the books they have decided are not Christian, urged on by their ministers. Anything that mentions ghosts, witches, spirits, has to go, and if that is taken literally, the Bible will have to be added to the pyre: because of Saul and the witch of Endor and Samuel's ghost. It reminds me a little of the hysteria during Joseph McCarthy's wild attempt to point his trembling finger at communists in this country. Not that there aren't communists in this country, working for our overthrow; there are. But when we get hysterical about it, we tend to start looking under the wrong beds; we ignore the dangerous people and begin to persecute the innocent. We seem to have learned nothing from Salem.

Recently I was sent a clipping from a midwestern newspaper listing ten books which were to be removed from the shelves because of their pornographic content. One of them was my own novel, *A Wind in the Door*. This has me both frankly fascinated and totally baffled. I have thought seriously about this, looking at the book to see if there is anything which could possibly be interpreted as pornographic, and haven't found anything. Another of the books cited was one of C. S. Lewis's Narnia Chronicles. This is the first time C. S. Lewis and I have been listed together as writers of pornography. Of course, if teenagers get hold of this list, the sales of our books will soar!

And that itself says something sad, not about the children, but about the world presented to them by the adults. We tend to find what we look for. If we have prurient minds, no matter how pure we delude ourselves into thinking we are, we will find pornography everywhere. If we are looking for dirt, we will find it, or worse, we will soil things which are not in themselves dirty. If we are looking for meaning, for order in complexity, for the love which heals, then we are less apt to find filth, seeing instead something which God has created, and is therefore valuable.

Some books, movies, paintings, are, in fact, destructively pornographic, and pornography is on the increase, in a world which we can no longer look on with loving eyes, seeing the goodness of it all. But C. S. Lewis pornographic? Should I laugh or cry?

Far worse than this absurdity is the sorry fact that all across the planet people who are convinced of the rightness of their religion are killing people whose religion differs from theirs. There seems to be a terrible confusion between faith and prejudice.

A young friend told me of an East Indian Christian who had suggested to her that we are not called to be Christians; we are called to be Christs. I find this both challenging and freeing when I am confused by all the things which Christians are doing all over the planet, in the name of Christ, which seem incompatible with all that Jesus taught.

I distrust the word *Christian* as an adjective; it has become less an adjective than a label, separating those who call themselves Christian from the rest of the world. How can those who would follow Christ assume that they are more beloved of the Creator than any other part of his creation, when God created *everything,* and saw that it was good? And if God created man in his own image, male and female, then all, *all* of humankind is part of that image, known or unknown, served or betrayed, accepted or denied. God loves every man, sings the psalmist. Perhaps it is more blessed to be aware of our part in the Image than not, but Jesus made it very clear that sometimes it is those who are least aware of it who serve the image best. It is truer to that image to be like the publican, aware of his unworthiness, than like the pharisee who was puffed up with the pride of his own virtue; it is truer to the image to say, "Lord, I believe; help thou my unbelief," than to dismiss the crucifixion by saying, "It is good for one man to die for the sake of the nation."

Faith consists in the acceptance of doubts, the working through them, rather than the repression of them.

Faith is beyond literal definition. If we could define it, or give a recipe for it, we could make a Fanny Farmer Cookbook of Faith, and all we'd have to do is check the index for the kind of faith we needed at the moment. But faith, like prayer, is a gift, a gift of knowing that the light shines in the darkness, of knowing that the light cannot be put out, no matter how diligently the tempter tries to snuff it. The gift, when it comes, frequently alters our perception of reality, and the manner in which we pray. Prayer, like faith, is a much misunderstood, much abused word. Sometimes we pray most honestly when we pray in ways which are considered childish, when we give ourselves to God just as we are, with all our imperfections, prejudices and faults. Is it really prayer when someone who cannot force us to change our honest point of view says, piously, "I'll pray for you"?

Throughout recorded history there have been totally different perceptions of reality. To the ancient Hebrews, a hierarchy of gods did not, for a long time, seem inconsistent with their *God is one and God is all*. The earth was the center of the universe, and the sun by day and the moon by night were put there entirely for our benefit. Community was not only understood, it was essential for survival, and when the ancient Hebrew said "I" it was seldom clear whether he meant himself as an individual or the community. There are examples of this equating of the person with the community in many of the psalms.

Communication with God was simple and direct and often startling. It would not have seemed as astounding then as it would be today to have the angel Gabriel appear to a young girl, hand her a lily, and tell her that she was going to become pregnant by the Holy Spirit.

But even by the time of this amazing event, the world view was far more complicated than it had been only a few centuries earlier; but we human beings, on planet earth, were still, and would continue to be for a good many more centuries, the prime focus of God's concern.

The mediaeval world, having gone through the harsh

purification of the Dark Ages, had its own clearly-dia-grammed perception of reality. Heaven was up; earth was here; hell was down. God's mysteries were taken for granted; and the relation between God and the creature was forthright. People were not afraid to ask God, *Why?*

In the Renaissance world the question became less *why* than *how?* This persistent asking of *how* can be seen in the notebooks of Leonardo da Vinci, although Leonardo, being a genius, often asked *why* and *how* at the same time.

As astronomy became a more and more sophisticated science, it was finally conceded that the earth was not, after all, the center of all that God had created, but a very small part of a greater whole—a difficult transition for many peo-ple. It is not easy for any of us to step out of the limelight.

With the coming of the industrial revolution and a focus on experiments which could be confirmed by laboratory testing, perceptions again shifted radically. When I was a school girl, probably the majority of scientists were atheists because God was no longer needed. Humanism rode high. It was assumed that what science had not yet discovered, it would shortly accomplish. We were, we thought, on the verge of knowing everything. The eating of the fruit of the tree of the knowledge of good and evil was about to pay off. The scientists in their labs, serene in the white coats of their priesthood, were the new gods.

I would like to think that it was my realization of this falseness that made me dislike math and science while I was in school, though if I had any such awareness it was purely intuitive and unknown to me. I loved geometry, because it dealt with questions, even when one was able to write Q.E.D. at the bottom of the paper. The rest of it I disliked because I was no good at it. During chemistry classes I tried to amuse myself by pretending that I was Madame Curie, and all I accomplished was blowing up the lab, which was in an old greenhouse. So when I am asked by interviewers about my "great scientific background," I have to reply that I have none. The magnificent theological mystery of science did not burst upon me until well after I was married and had three children.

Science changed, irrevocably, with the splitting of the atom, and our perception of reality has not yet caught up with this change. We discovered that for every question we have answered, a hundred new questions have been uncovered. For all our knowledge, all our technical advances, we have learned to our chagrin (and sometimes delight) that we know practically nothing.

We are still in the process of tiptoeing over the sill of this new perception of the universe which is, strangely, far more like the universe in which Abraham and Sarah found themselves when they left home and went into a strange land, than it is like the exalted individualism of Renaissance man, or the technocratic smugness of the late nineteenth and early twentieth centuries.

Our contemporary mystics are the astrophysicists, the cellular biologists, the physicists who study quantum mechanics, for they are dealing with the nature of being itself. Like Abraham and Sarah they are continually discovering the extraordinary mystery of being, and the charting of the worlds within us as well as the worlds beyond us. And we, too, are being asked to leave our comfortable home and go out into the wilderness, like Abraham and Sarah, into the mysterious world of unknown spaces, where there may be famine, drought, hostile inhabitants.

Only one thing was certain in Abraham's and Sarah's uncertain world, only one thing stands sure in ours, and that is that the universe is God's. Out of nothing el created us, and called us into being that we might go out into the unknown and become co-creators with our Creator, in this new and uncharted land where our concepts of space and time are radically different from what they were half a century ago.

So, as always in the face of the unknown, I turn and return to story. The first of the great stories in the Bible is that of Adam and Eve. The point is not which came first, the chicken or the egg, but that it is not good for the human being to be alone. Each of us needs others. Any single one of us, alone, cannot be the image of God; discovering that image within us is not a do-it-yourself activity. Before I can be an icon of the image of God, I must be with someone else, hand in hand.

As there are two creation stories in Genesis, so there are two stories of the making of Adam and Eve, and both make the same point. Despite the proliferation of do-it-yourself books, we can't do it ourselves. We need each other. As to who came first, Jesus makes it very clear that this is a matter of unimportance. He emphasizes this by stating that the first shall be last, and the last shall be first. Adam is not better than Eve because he arrived on the scene first; nor is Eve less than Adam because she came second. (Often the butler and the maid begin the play.) It was the story-teller's realization that it is not good for the human creature to be alone that is important. God has called us to be co-creators, a corporate activity. Dean Inge of St. Paul's says, "God promised to make you free. He never promised to make you independent."

We are most free when we are most willing to acknowledge our interdependence. Adam and Eve were free until they saw each other as separate and autonomous, and afraid of their Creator.

———◆◆———

We never pray alone. Ever. Even if there is no other human being around us who is willing or able to pray with us, we are in the company of angels and archangels. We are surrounded by a glorious cloud of witnesses. And, even when we feel most isolated, there *are* other human creatures, somewhere, who are praying with us. It used to be required in my church that we read morning and evening prayer, and although it is no longer required, not even for those who are ordained, I am grateful that many of us still find comfort in this daily structure, so that when I am praying in this manner I know that many thousands of people are praying with me. A quiet listening to the words of the Psalms, to the readings from both Old and New Testaments, to the great prayers of the collects and canticles, is often a prelude to the prayers which go beyond words, go deeper than words, leading us from reading to thinking to prayer. And the practice of morning and evening prayer provides a structure to the day which keeps everything in proportion and perspective.

In the spring of the year I am among those who give the oral examinations to candidates for ordination who have already gone through most of the process. They have finished seminary, taken their General Ordination examinations, and are nearly ready for ordination in the Episcopal Church. Our job, in my diocese, is to examine these young men and women in whatever subject they have shown the greatest weakness.

This spring I was examining with two priests who are friends of mine, and with whom I am easy and comfortable and can speak spontaneously. Among those who came to us for examination was a personable young man who had done well throughout seminary and on his exams, but who showed a slight weakness in pastoral concerns. I asked him something I usually ask: "What are your own personal disciplines of prayer?" He replied that whenever it was possible he liked to read morning prayer, but that often he was so busy that there was no time. "All it takes is ten minutes!" I exclaimed. "Why don't you read it on the john?"

To my amazement, I had shocked him. He asked, "But isn't that sacrilegious?"

Almost equally shocked by this response, I said, "That is a very unincarnational question."

One of my priest friends reminded him that Luther had done some deep theological thinking on what, in his day, was called the jakes, and all three of us tried to get over to him that life cannot be separated into secular and sacred, that if God created everything, and called it good, then all of life is good, and only we can see it as sacrilegious. There is nothing which is, of itself, sacrilegious. Just as the act of making love can be sacramental, so can all aspects of our lives, even the most lowly. If we cannot pray in the bathroom, it is not likely that we will be able to pray anywhere.

My suggestion came not out of thin air but out of my own experience. Sometimes when I am on a lecture tour I am so tightly scheduled that there is certainly no programmed time for my reading of morning and evening prayer. But I need the affirmation and the structure they give me, and often the only time and place is in the bathroom. How can it be sacrilegious? God is the Lord of all of all my life, and there is no place where it is not proper to turn to my Maker.

Paul said it so cogently in his first letter to Corinth:

Those parts of the body which seem to us to be less deserving of notice we have to allow the highest honor of function. The parts which do not look beautiful have a deeper beauty in the work they do, while the parts which look beautiful may not be at all essential to life!

In the Garden of Eden there was no separation of sacred and secular; separation is one of the triumphs of the devil. All of creation is God's, and therefore it is all sacred. And when everything is sacred, then we can understand something about freedom.

Part of the meaning of the incarnation is that Jesus en-Christed everything, giving it again the sacredness it had when the Word first spoke all of creation into being.

God created Adam in a sacred world in which it was truly possible to be free. God made Adam, and saw that it was not good for this creature to be alone, and so God gave Adam a helpmeet. It is a marvellous story, and it tells us a great deal about the nature of ourselves and our relationship to God.

Story, unlike theories of science which are always open to change, is timeless. The story of Adam and Eve may have different things to say to different generations in different places, but it always has something to say. Therefore it touches on the nature of reality.

Once again we come to the old question: what is real? I look at my hand, at the bones and veins and skin, at the fingers which can touch the keys of the typewriter and so put words on paper, or touch the keys of a piano, and bring the sounds of a fugue or a sonata into the room. I rub them together and I can feel them generating a healing electricity. I take a whisk in one hand, hold the pot with the other, and stir eggs and butter and lemon juice to make hollandaise sauce. My hands are very real to me. And yet I know that they are also a whirling dance of electrons, and that there are vast spaces between the parts of the electrons. There is energy in my hands, and energy and matter are interchangeable. The movement of my hands is not contained within the skin and bone, muscle and nerve, but is triggered by that part of my brain which is focused on the movement of my hands, my fingers. There is far more that I do not know about my hands than that I know. But they are real. I don't understand their reality, but neither do I doubt it.

If Pontius Pilate did not know what truth was, neither did he know reality, and most of us aren't much further along the way than he. God creates from nothing, *ex nihilo*, but we, el's creatures, can create only from what el has already created and given us. Therefore our reality must be part of God's reality if it is to have any validity. Could Shakespeare have created Hamlet if such a character were not possible? Isn't the perennial fascination with Hamlet partly because we all see something of ourselves in this questioning creature, and partly because Hamlet, like the rest of us, is so complex that he can never be understood? But is Hamlet unreal?

I had a delightful letter from a woman who expressed her hope that after death she would meet some of her favorite fictional characters. I agree with her that this would be a delightful aspect of heaven. There are so many I would like to meet—Emily of New Moon, Ivan Karamazov, Mole and Rat, Viola and Duke Orsino, Mary Lennox, and even, I hope, some of the characters who have come to me in my own books.

So story is real. And music is real, and what is real is an icon of our Creator, even if some of us who have been wounded balk at the use of the word, *Father*. A Bach fugue is for me an icon of this reality, and so with my often inadequate fingers I struggle at the piano, in order to get myself back into reality.

And when I go to a museum I am not going just to look at an exhibition of painting or sculpture in order to be *au courant* with the latest cultural fashion; I am going in order to look for that reality which will help me to live my own life more fully, more courageously, more freely.

So there is no doubt in my mind that Adam and Eve are real.

And one of the first things their story points out is the importance of Naming.

(Here we go again: Madeleine and Naming. She's like a dog with a bone. True. But anyone who has had a name taken away, as happened to me in boarding school when, at age twelve, I was numbered, 97, not Madeleine, is likely to be overconcerned on the subject of names. Can we be over-concerned? Granted, naming seems to crop up in every-thing I write, but that is because it cannot, in this day of uninvolved anonymity, be overemphasized.)

All the animals, all the fish and fowl and land beasts had to be named in order to be. And we cannot name ourselves alone. Before we can love each other, before we can dia-logue, each one of us has to be named by the other and we have to name in return.

While Adam and Eve were naming the animals, the story is that Adam asked, "Hey, Eve, why are you calling that creature a hippopotamus?"

And Eve replied, "Because it *looks* like a hippo-potamus."

Are we going to be able to remain God's creatures who are known by name? On our little ship we could not be-come friends with any of our fellow passengers until we had exchanged names. "Hello, we are Hugh and Madeleine." Until we were Hugh and Madeleine we were not quite real. Can you imagine saying to someone, "Hello, I'm 061-12-5619." That's Hugh's social security number, which he has memorized, so when anyone asks, "What's your social security number?" he is able to rattle it off. But it's not his name. *I* call him Hugh.

I do not know my social security number. I have no intention of ever knowing my social security number. I can look it up if absolutely necessary. But if we don't take care, if we don't watch out, society may limit us to numbers. I wonder if I could pray if I lost my name? I am not at all sure that I could.

If we are numbered, not named, we are less than human. One of the most terrible things done to slaves throughout the centuries, from Babylon to Rome to the United States, was to take away their names. Isn't one of the worst things we can do to any prisoner to take away his name or her name and call them by numbers? If you take away someone's name, you can treat that person as a thing with a clear conscience. You can horsewhip a thing far more easily than a person with a name, a name known to you. No wonder the people who were put in Nazi concentration camps had numbers branded on their arms.

When Adam named the animals he made them real. My dog is named Timothy and my cat is named Titus. Farmers do not let their children name the animals who are going to be slaughtered or put in the pot. It is not easy to eat a ham you have known as Wilbur or a chicken called Flossy.

When we respond to our names, or call someone else by name, it is already the beginning of a community expressing the image of God. To call someone by name is an act of prayer. We may abuse our names, and our prayer, but without names we are not human. And Adam and Eve, no matter what else they were, were human.

At first there was nothing but joy, joy in being created, and in worshiping the God who had created them. And wonder: wonder at sunrises and starfish and dolphin and even dandelions. My husband, who mows the lawn at Crosswicks, hates dandelions, but they are indeed wondrous things, and not to be taken for granted. In early June the big hay field north of our house is white with dandelion clocks, and the prevailing north-westerly winds blow those incredibly productive dandelions clocks right onto our lawn. My husband takes this insult so personally that I am not allowed to put delicious young dandelion greens into the salad. But he does not take dandelions for granted.

Abraham Joshua Heschel says: "The surest way to suppress our ability to understand the meaning of God and the importance of worship is *to take things for granted.* Indifference to the sublime wonder of being is the root of sin."

Were Adam and Eve beginning to take the image of God in themselves and the loveliness of Eden for granted? Is that why they fell for Satan's temptations?

When we take things for granted, then what we have is not enough, and we are rendered vulnerable to the wiles of the tempter. We tend to take our own democratic freedom for granted, and every time I leave this country, especially if I am going to Asia or to South America, I am jolted to a fresh awareness of just how fortunate we are, despite all of the things which are wrong and getting worse. And I wonder anew at our funny, fumbling system, which nevertheless gives us freedoms unknown to people in countries with restrictions we find it hard to conceive of.

If Adam and Eve had remained satisfied, joyous and grateful for all the wonders of creation, for the creatures they had named, for the beauty of Eden, they would not have listened to the tempter, who came to them with the same temptations he offered Jesus: if you do what I say, you can be as God. *You can be God.*

When we lose our sense of wonder we become dissatisfied with who we are (just as the tempter became dissatisfied with who he was, the most luminous of all the angels); like the tempter, we are no longer content to be created. To love God and enjoy him forever begins to be dull. We are ripe for temptation.

———◆◆———

It is my great good fortune to have for a close friend a woman who is as tall as I am, who was as gawky an adolescent as I was, who sees herself, as she says, as a mouse, but who is the chief health officer of a great city. We have known each other since we were in our late teens, and we have done a lot of growing up together, falling over many of the same stumbling blocks, and picking ourselves up out of the mud, wiping off the blood, and stumbling on. In the late summer she visits us at Crosswicks, and we go into a massive apple-sauce factory production. A couple of summers ago we were in the midst of the sauce pot and the Foley food mill when our corner of Connecticut was hit by the fringe of a hurricane. The rain and wind were lashing the house when the power went out and we ran out of apples. Without even consulting each other we ran upstairs, put on our bathing suits, and dashed out into the storm to pick more apples, exhilarated by the deluge of rain against our skin and the apples falling from the trees as the wind whipped the branches. Later on I thought how marvellous it is to have a friend, also in her sixties, with whom I can be so foolish and so gloriously happy, full of wonder at the marvel of being. And this sense of wonder is also prayer.

It is this awareness of the marvellousness of creation which helps to keep dissatisfaction away; rejoicing in and being wholly satisfied with being God's co-creators is a prayer of protection.

To be dissatisfied with who we are is not the same thing as that divine discontent which Plato talks about. Divine discontent is to accept to our sorrow that we are *not* what we have been created to be. We have fallen far short of our small part in the image of God; we are *less* than we are. Once we are aware of this we can open ourselves to our Creator, saying, Help me to be what you want me to be.

Whereas being dissatisfied with who we are involves being dissatisfied with being created. We have been given a marvellous role in the great drama, and suddenly it is not enough. But we become discontented with our roles and want our name up on the marquee in brighter and larger lights than anybody else's.

Adam and Eve lost their joy, their radical amazement at the wonders of being, simply being, being Adam and Eve, being Namers. They no longer looked at the world around them and said,

This is the Lord's doing; it is marvellous in our eyes.

And in came the tempter.

"It's all right," he said. "You can do anything you want to, you know."

When you've stopped being delighted with who you are, it's very nice to be told you're special. Even if there's nobody else around to be more special *than,* it's still a pleasurable feeling.

After that we are ripe for the real temptation. "Do as I tell you: eat the apple; jump from the highest pinnacle of the temple; worship me, and you shall be as God."

Hubris. Usurping the prerogatives of God.

"Go on then," the tempter urged. "You won't die if you eat the fruit of the forbidden tree. The only reason el doesn't want you to eat it is that el knows that if you do, you'll be able to tell right from wrong, and then you'll be as God."

So they ate of the fruit of the tree of the knowledge of

good and evil, and the timing was all off; they weren't ready, and so the result was confusion.

Ever since that first disastrous mistiming, we have grown in knowledge without being aware that we have not grown equally in spirit. Children are pushed, and themselves push, to grow up earlier and earlier. We have forgotten that time is a creature like us, and that our relation with time is of the utmost importance. Adam and Eve knew too much before they had grown enough to be ready for knowledge. It was something like offering a double martini to a two-year-old; urging a five-year-old to read Freud; giving unleashed electricity to a ten-year-old. Adam and Eve were incapable of assimilating all that they suddenly knew. They saw that they were naked, and in their beautiful, created bodies they were embarrassed, not because they were cold, but because without preparation they suddenly knew more than they could possibly understand. And of course Satan sees pornography everywhere.

He must have known that when they ate the forbidden fruit they weren't going to be like God at all. They weren't even going to be like the human beings they were.

The Light
in the
Darkness

4

How was it that the Prince of Light became the Prince of Darkness?

We are all meant to be light-bearers, but for Lucifer it was not enough to bear the light. Long before the Garden, Lucifer wanted to *be* the Light, and, in that passionate desire he lost the light by falling into the darkness of hubris. Now there is a touch of it in all of us, for we bear, as a wound, the sins of our ancestors.

We are not willing to bear the light. We want to be the Light. We want to be God. But what kind of God? Like Lucifer? Full of earthly power and grandeur, able to wave wands and work magic, reaching out greedily for the things of this world?

This is the god that Jesus rejected when the Holy Spirit led him into the wilderness to be tempted. And so he went not to a royal, temporal throne, but to the cross.

Adam and Eve did not live long enough to understand that the cross is the gateway to heaven. Most of us don't understand that, either, and so, like Adam and Eve, we bicker, we quarrel, we alibi, we jostle for power and glory.

A news letter was distributed on our freighter every morning, and every morning it was bad news, hijackers, assassinations, wars accumulating all over the planet in the name of religion: Islam, Judaism, Christianity, Communism . . .

There is little difference between communism and some of the extreme sects which demand the total subservience of their followers. Questions are forbidden. Life is easier when no questions are asked, when all behavioural patterns are dictated. Within the structure that restricts rather than the structure that frees we lose our ability to make choices. But if we make no choices, we lose our creativity, we lose touch with real life, we lose more of the image of God, we abdicate our own human nature.

Granted, the ability to make choices does not automatically mean that we will make the right choices, otherwise what kind of real choice would it be? Since that first wrong choice made by Adam and Eve, when the timing of the human psyche got out of sync, we have continued to make disastrously wrong choices. For all our technocratic advances we have not been able to control terrorism, which grows worse daily. We have not stopped war. We see all around us the results of corruption and greed.

Sometimes we see in small ways, almost more clearly than in the great, the sick results of the accumulation of wrong choices. When I am in New York I start the day by filling my thermos with coffee, taking my old Irish setter, Timothy, and heading for the Cathedral library. As I walk I say my memorized alphabet of prayers, which helps clear my mind of trivialities. In the morning as I come to the words "... because in the mystery of the Word made flesh..." I look at whomever is nearest me so that I may see in that person, for that moment, Christ. The upper west side of Broadway is a heterogeneous neighborhood, and I may see a wino, a child going to school, the young, the old, the indigent.

That morning I saw an old black man carrying a large, plastic bag. When he saw me and my dog, this "Christ" took the plastic bag and began hitting at the dog and me with it. I said, as I might have said to one of my children, "Please, don't do that," and then, in a loud voice, without thinking, just saying it, "Christ help you." At that point his bag broke and bottles flew all over the sidewalk, shattering, and he careened away from the frightened dog and me. I walked on, soothing the quivering setter, my legs stinging from the assault, and a doorman, who was out hosing his sidewalk and who had been about to intervene, asked, "Is he mad?"

"Out of his mind," I replied, and walked on, too shaken even to talk. But, no matter how crazed he was, that man had to be Christ for me. If I cannot see Christ in the maimed, in those possessed by devils, I cannot see Christ in the whole and holy. But that was, in its own way, a small act of terrorism. And the greater acts of terrorism increase, too, as all the little gods in South America or South Africa or behind the iron curtain or in our own country play the game of god more and more frantically.

We can't undo what Adam and Eve did. We have more knowledge than the human mind can cope with, and we can't make it go away—and we don't want it to go away. It is not the knowledge which is the problem, but our misuse of it.

How ironic it is that we're still far from having the knowledge of good and evil, and it is more difficult to distinguish between them today than it was in Eden. Daily the nations' leaders, and we ourselves in smaller ways, are faced with decisions, with choices where there is no clear-cut answer. Should a baby conceived in rape be carried to term or aborted? To the fourteen-year-old girl who has been brutally raped, is the psychological damage greater if she has to carry the child of this horror for nine months, or if it is taken from her body as soon as possible? Abortion is murder, but there are times when the death of the fetus would seem to bring less evil than if it were not sent back to God as quickly as possible.

Children are always hurt by divorce. Yet sometimes they are more hurt if parents with an unendurable marriage stay together. There are no easy answers. Often we are put in positions where all of our choices are wrong; there is no *right* thing to do. At that point we must pray that we choose that which is least evil, and then ask for forgiveness for that inevitable evil which we have done.

Satan cannot make us like God. He promised it in Eden, he promises it now, but he cannot fulfill that promise. He can only make us like himself, carrying hell with him, being, in himself, hell.

We are not meant to be like Satan; we are meant to be like God, to be God's creatures, bearing el's image, making that image visible as we come together in community, the community of friendship, of marriage, of the church—the body of Christ. We are far more than we know, and even when we fall desperately short of that which we were meant to be, we are children by adoption and grace. When Adam and Eve left Eden, they were God's children. Even bickering, blaming each other, rationalizing and alibi-ing, they were still God's children. They could no longer walk and talk with their maker when el walked in the evening in the cool of the garden; but even though they could not see el, the Lord was there, watching them, caring.

Knowledge without wisdom can be a terrible thing. Now when Adam and Eve knew each other, they knew that they knew.

They knew each other, and Eve became pregnant and bore Cain.

That first birth has always fascinated me. When I was just out of college and living alone in Greenwich Village in New York, struggling to make a living as a writer and making it mostly as a general understudy and assistant stage manager in the theatre, I wrote the following tale:

The First Birth

"Adam," she said, "I'm afraid. Something strange has happened to me." She lay under the tree, staring up into his eyes. The roots of the tree were old and round, and seemed to be holding her body in strong, impersonal arms.

Adam dropped to his knees and held out a handful of berries. "Eat. Maybe you'll feel better then."

She sighed deeply in her fear and shook her head at the berries. "I'm not hungry. Only thirsty. What I want is some coconut milk. Would you..."

Still down on his knees Adam looked at her. "You forget," he said. "There are no coconut trees here. Only there..."

"But I want coconut milk. If only I had some I think I'd feel better."

"It's not my fault you can't have coconut milk, you know," Adam said.

Tears welled in her eyes; her fingers tightened on the round coarse arm of tree root; she dug her toes into the rough, dry moss. For some reason she did not want Adam to see her cry. After a long time, when she was sure her voice would come steadily, she said, "Something very

71

strange has happened to me. Something I don't understand. Something we didn't learn when we had to leave home. Perhaps this is learning about death. I don't want to learn about death."

Adam bent over her, slipping his fingers under the antelope skin she was wearing, and felt her round, distended stomach. "It seems even larger," he said.

"Sometimes when I am holding it I feel something moving inside, as though something were striking me. Is this another way of His showing His anger?"

"No," Adam said. "I don't think He would punish us twice for one thing."

"Please, Adam," she whispered, "if I could only have some coconut milk."

"All right," he said. "I'll try. I'll try and slip in somehow. But if I don't get back you'll know He has killed me."

"Don't get killed, Adam!" she almost shrieked, clutching at his tunic of elk-hide and pulling him towards her.

"You can be so unreasonable..." he sighed. "First you want me to go get you coconut milk then you don't want me to get killed when you know perfectly well what He said about our trying to get back. Well, I'll try to get the coconut milk and I'll try not to get killed, and if that doesn't satisfy you I don't know what will." And he got up from his knees, the little bits of moss and twig sticking to them making a fine tracery on his brown skin. But before he had gone more than a few yards he turned and came back. She was lying there with her eyes closed, paying no attention to a dry green leaf of the tree that had floated down and lay tickling against her bare right shoulder. Tears were slowly streaming from under her heavy lids. Again Adam got down onto his knees, bent over her, and pressed his lips against hers. Without opening her eyes she reached out and held him to her, her fingers as strong as though she were clutching him in pain.

72

"I hurt," she whispered.

Against his tongue he tasted the salt wetness of her tears. Her hair was moist where the tears had rolled unchecked, and he pushed it back from her face, clumsily, trying to dry her cheeks with the palm of his hand, but succeeding only in leaving streaks of dirt. "I'll hurry," he said, stood up, and ran off through the trees.

After the trees came a field of waving yellow grasses and after the grasses a river. This he swam, then clambered up a stony hill. Up, up, until the stones gave way to green clumps of bushes, until the bushes gave way to stones again, and the stones in their place to snow. From the top of the hill where ice cold rock had taken the place of the snow he could see their old home. A pang of desire went into his heart that was similar to the pang he had felt when his lips first touched Eve's that night they left home; and they had fallen together, rolling over and over on the ground. That had been a feeling that had momentarily made them forget that they must leave their home forever, that had made their life as eternal refugees seem bearable and even preferable to the old. Now as he saw the green peace of home again he forgot everything else, forgot even Eve, forgot everything but the great tidal wave of homesickness that swept over him and threw him down sobbing on the icy grey coldness of rock. The rock was so cold that it froze his sobs in his throat, kept the tears from coming out of his anguished eyes. He pulled himself up onto his knees, stretched his arms out until every muscle in his body was tightened to its utmost extreme, and cried out in a voice so deep that if he had been able to hear it, it would have made him afraid, *"Please!"* Then with a great struggle he managed to scramble back onto his feet and start running, tumbling, plunging down the mountainside.

But when he had come near enough to home to feel in

his lungs and against his cheek the difference in the air, to smell and almost to taste the difference, he saw, in a great flash of lightning, the angel with the flaming sword at the gates. Then there was a crash of thunder and he was flat on the ground, the dirt grinding against his teeth. When the thunder finally stopped reverberating in his ears he realized that he was in darkness such as he had never known. This was not the darkness he and Eve had found the night they left home and lay in each other's arms the whole of that first night. This was not a darkness tempered by stars, or even a night of clouds with a moon hidden somewhere in the depths. This was not a night of fireflies darting or of glow worms' slow light. This was a darkness such as he had never known. If it had not been for the taste of dirt in his mouth he would not have known that it was the familiar earth that he was lying on; he would have thought that this darkness that was so intense somehow had shape and solidity, had the power to hold him up; or perhaps he was falling through it, plunging downwards headlong like an unlighted comet. Only the grating of dirt against his teeth reassured him that the world was still there, that he was still alive. Even if the sun or moon or stars had been near he felt that their light could not possibly have penetrated this darkness that lay upon him with such heaviness that it seemed as though it was breaking his bones, pressing his ribs together.

Nothing could pierce this darkness but sound, and out of its depths came a voice:

"Move On!"

It was a voice of many trumpets, a voice of the singing of stars, of the clashing of armies, and storms of the skies, a voice that was light dispelling the darkness.

At first as the blackness was slow in lifting he crawled along on his stomach like the snake. Then as he began to see

74

through a thick grey fog, on his hands and knees; and at last as he neared the top of the mountain on his homeward journey and the sky lay streaked with blood on the horizon, he stood and began to run.

When he got back Eve was still lying under the tree, dirt streaked on her face where he had tried to dry her tears; but she was no longer on her back in languid weariness. She had rolled onto her side; with her hands she was clutching the tree roots and she was writhing back and forth, moaning.

Adam dropped beside her. He did not tell her of the angel with the flaming sword or the night that had come on him like a thunder clap. "I couldn't get the coconut milk."

But she had forgotten the coconut milk. When she realized that he was there she loosed her grasp on the tree roots and transferred it to him. Once he felt her teeth sink into his shoulder but somehow it didn't hurt and he felt only a strange satisfaction as he saw the red blood running down his arm. Then her grip slowly relaxed and she lay exhausted in his arms. Her antelope skin was wringing with cold sweat and when he laid his hand on her distended stomach she screamed because the pains were starting again.

They had never seen a baby before. It lay there between them in a bed shaped by the roots of the tree, and screamed at them angrily. It was very red and wrinkled. Its open mouth from which issued such ferocious yowls held no teeth. The eyelids which were squeezed close shut were seamed with a thousand wrinkles. They knew that it looked older than anything they had ever seen before.

"This is what we will look like when we are to learn about death," Adam whispered.

Eve suddenly snatched up the little starfish and held it to her. She had lost the antelope skin somewhere in the midst of her pains but she was unconscious of this now. She only knew that she must hold this little thing to her and somehow keep it safe.

"But what is it?" Adam whispered.

"I don't know, but you had better go get it a skin to keep it warm at night."

Adam stood undecidedly looking down at them. "You don't hurt any more?"

She laughed. "I had forgotten all about it!"

"You had forgotten!" he exclaimed in astonishment. He could never forget the feeling of her teeth sinking into his shoulder, her antelope skin wringing wet with cold, her face dead white with a circle of transparent green about the mouth, the nostrils pinched, the eyes glazed and sightless, and bestial animal sounds issuing from deep in her throat. All this he would remember when he was an old man with white hair.

"I had forgotten all about it!" she laughed. And then said in a voice that was tremulous with ecstasy, "But Adam, it was wonderful! I would do it again!"

He looked at her, disgust and anger rising in him. "You hurt and you forget it," he said heavily. "Something that it seems to me must be bad you say is good. How can something good come of hurt and badness?"

She laughed again. "I don't know, but this is good."

He scowled down at the little thing in her arms and strode off. Eve hardly noticed his going. She sat there, leaning back against the trunk of the tree, for she was exhausted with an exhaustion she had never known before, quite different from the feeling she had had the night they left home and set out to find a new place for themselves. This was an exhaustion that was wholly pleasant. She lay back against the tree, and the little screaming starfish in her arms suddenly became quiet and relaxed, drooping against her. She rocked it back and forth, her eyes closed, singing, murmuring over and over again, "Little old age, little old Adam, little knowledge of death," without realizing that she was using words or tune.

By and by she became conscious of a hissing. Opening her eyes slowly she saw the serpent, his hood spread, his little forked tongue quivering, stretching towards her. She snatched her child away, but not before the serpent had licked one small hand with its tongue, leaving a long red mark. Terror sprang into her heart.

"You go away!"

The serpent coiled around and writhed at her insinuatingly. "You thought me beautiful once. Let me just see your child. I can tell you all about your child."

"Go away, snake!" she shrieked. Still holding the baby in one arm, with the other she picked up the largest stone that she could manage, a boulder much greater than she would have attempted to lift with both arms ordinarily, and heaved it at the serpent, who writhed out of its path and slid away through the underbrush while the stone pounded down hill. When Eve was certain he was not coming back again, she sank down against the tree, exhausted. The child had begun to cry, raising its voice in a long, thin wail, and she sat clutching it to her until her heart had ceased its pounding and she could sing to it again without a tremor of terror in her voice.

When Adam returned with the skin, a very small skin, the child was sucking at her breast, while she rocked back and forth ever so slightly, ever so gently, singing. He threw the skin down at her feet; then, as she looked up at him, smiling, with an expression he had never seen on her face before, he flung himself down beside her, pressing his face against her thigh because he knew she would not allow him to disturb the little creature at her breast, and burst into a perfect passion of tears because of this day which had been the most terrible day of his life.

Thus far. For surely Cain was to give Adam far greater pain later on than he did on the day of his birth.

When Abel was conceived it must have been easier. Eve would have understood what was going on inside her body. She would have realized that her swollen breasts held milk for the infant.

If it was difficult to bear the first child, it must have been even more difficult to *be* the first child. And to be the cause of the first death.

Cain killed Abel. And that was the beginning. Brother against brother. Yankees killing Southerners and Southerners killing Yankees. Puritans killing Roundheads and Roundheads killing Puritans. Protestants killing Catholics and Catholics killing Protestants. Moslems. Christians, Jews, Cain killing Abel... will it ever stop?

Intersecting
Circles
5

WHEN I WAS WRITING that old story of Adam and Eve, I was both Adam and Eve. And I am also Cain and Abel. Scripture is not only the living Word of God, it is also my story, and your story. In the pages of Genesis, and all through the Bible, we recognize ourselves. It is God showing us who we are, and who el wants us to be. If we are to have the courage to recognize ourselves as God reveals us to ourselves, we must have the courage to face ourselves, not only the parts which we like or of which we approve.

The story of Adam and Eve, of their making, of their expulsion from the Garden of Eden into a world so much less real that it was almost unendurable, of the birth of their children, is in its symbolic way a blueprint of our own personalities. Each of us will recognize something different, but if we are honest, each of us will recognize something of ourselves.

In a book on Jung by Laurens van der Post I read with awe of Jung's feeling that we have completely misunderstood the Roman Catholic doctrine of the Assumption of the Virgin Mary. We have interpreted it literally instead of mythically. For, Jung points out, what this doctrine is really doing is attempting to return the feminine to the Godhead.

And I thought: How stupid I've been! Falling for the old trap of literal-mindedness again.

Perhaps this urge to literal-mindedness is why we pay so comparatively little attention to the Holy Spirit as an equal part of the unity of the Trinity, even in the most charismatic settings. Somehow it does not help to affirm the feminine aspect of the Godhead, or the Holy Spirit elself, by saying "She"—because the concept is far deeper than a personal pronoun.

Though the Holy Spirit calls forth from us all that is nurturing and intuitive, there is also a wildness of which we are afraid, and so we tend to suppress it. The wind of the Spirit can be balmy and tender, but it can also be fierce, can lash waves to mountainous heights, can become a tornado which creates destruction in its path. We rightly equate the Holy Spirit with wind—the word for spirit is the same as the word for wind in Hebrew: *ruach*.

This wildness is the maternal aspect of the Trinity!

Some people (and I have encountered this feeling in both the male and female of the species, but more often in the male) see the maternal being as totally devouring. The mother wants to eat the child, they say, and so the mother must be killed.

What must be killed, I think, is the false image of the mother we have created. Needing something to blame, we invent an image of the parent which often has no resemblance to reality. And we do need to kill this image in order to be able to love whomever is the real mother.

Let us not blame this image-making and mother-killing entirely on the male. One young woman told me that her relations with her mother were not good, yet her mother always knew when something was wrong, and would call her. She would try to pretend that everything was all right, because she didn't want her mother to be worried; she felt that she had to protect her mother. I told her that perhaps she needed to "kill" her mother, in order to be able to share with the real person, whose intuitive love did not need to be protected from whatever was troubling her daughter.

As both a daughter and a mother, I know how dangerous our images of our mothers can be. But we are hardier than we realize.

I am grateful for Jung's insight. It caused me to remember that Meister Eckhart, and many other mystics, have the same disregard for the limitations of sex. Eckhart writes: "The soul will bring forth Person if God laughs into her and she laughs back to him."

We need a little more merriment and considerably less brittleness as we come face to face with the problems of human and divine sexuality.

Since we are sexual human beings, we cannot avoid thinking about the Adam or the Eve in us. I doubt that it is possible for us to think about God without at least a touch of anthropomorphism (at least as long as our humanity limits as well as releases us). Throughout the centuries all people have wanted to know what God looks like. I am frequently amazed at how many people visualize God as looking like Moses—and Moses in a bad temper, at that. But the God of the Old Testament, the God to whom Jesus remained true, was, and is, slow to anger, quick to forgive, caring about recalcitrant human beings, longing for us to turn to our Maker, to love our Creator, to receive el's compassionate love. All through the Old Testament el participates in crea-

tion, and in the destiny of each of el's creatures. So the ultimate participation, God's becoming one of us in Jesus, is no
surprise.

We're in it together, and God is in it, with us.

When our children were little, we had long bedtimes,
stories, songs, prayers. And when things happened which
were hard for us to comprehend like a sudden and unexpected death, I would pile the children into the station
wagon and drive up to the top of Mohawk Mountain, to the
fire-lookout tower, and we would lie on the great, flat glacial
rocks and watch the stars come out, and talk about whatever
it was that had shocked or hurt us. I'm not sure where the
idea came from that all of creation is God's body, but if we
must have an analogy, it is not a bad one.

When I look at the galaxies on a clear night—when I
look at the incredible brilliance of creation, and think that
this is what God is like, then, instead of feeling intimidated
and diminished by it, I am enlarged—I rejoice that I am
part of it, I, you, all of us—part of this glory. And so, when
we go to the altar to receive the bread and wine, we are
taking into our own bodies all of creation, all of the galaxies.
And our total interdependence is an astounding glory.

We are whatever we eat—junk foods, well-balanced
meals, the books we ingest, the people we listen to—but
most marvellously we are the eternally loving power of creativity. Does it sound incredible to say that when we receive
Communion we are eating the entire universe? Of course it
does, but it is also incredibly possible, and I rejoice in it.

As for size—as the old southern phrase has it, size
makes no never mind. Those two sources of radio emission,
sending their messages across millions of light years, are as
close together as the eyes in a beloved face. A grain of sand
commands as much respect as a galaxy. A flower is as bright
as the sun. But all, all are part of creation. So, as there is

nothing we can do that does not affect someone else (we can never truthfully say "it's my own business"), there is nothing we can do that does not affect God. This is an awesome responsibility, and one which we offer and accept whenever we receive Communion, asking that we may dwell in God and he in us.

This is not, as some people have wrongly assumed, magic. It is faith that God made everything, and that el saw that it was good. Nothing can be separated from God's love, or from the Word without which nothing was made that was made.

When I look at the stars to help me find perspective, I am seeking an alternate reality, one which is deeper and more real than the world of immediate consciousness.

Different people have different perceptions of reality, and our own perceptions change as we move from infancy to childhood to adolescence to adulthood. As Americans, as people whose background is from the Judeo-Christian tradition, the terms of our reality are very different from that of a fundamentalist Muslim whose presuppositions involve bloodbaths and the ritual killing of anyone who disagrees. But to someone within the framework of this reality, his is right, and ours is wrong. Can we be sure we are right? What about the Spanish Inquisition, the burning of anyone accused of being a witch, even if the accusation was false?

We have strayed far from the reality of those peoples of the world who live close to the land, who listen to the language of the birds, the singing of the trees, the message of the clouds in the sky. Our loss.

We are far from the reality of many of the people we encounter every day. I am light years away from the perception of reality of people who find that story is a lie, who believe that to act in a play is a sin, because it is to "make believe," and who have fallen for one of the devil's cleverest deceptions, that myth is not a vehicle of truth, but a falsehood.

Like it or not, we each live within our own perception of reality which makes each one of us the center of our particular universe. Some of the thoughts I have just been expressing have come from the overlapping of my own reality with that of the authors of two books I have been reading, *Alternate Realities*, by Lawrence le Shan, and *A Story Like the Wind*, by Laurens van der Post. The idea that we are each one the center of the universe has been haunting me for a long time, not because it seems a selfish idea of reality; it need not be; but because it can sometimes narrow our understanding of interdependence, and the necessity for the circles of our realities to overlap. I had even written this down, thinking it was a wholly original idea of mine, and then, as so often happens, the next morning I came to a question in le Shan's book by Thomas Mann: (I have used language somewhat more contemporary than the translator.)

> The world has many centers, one for each created being, and about each one lies his own circle. You stand but half an ell from me, and yet about you lies a universe whose center I am not, but you are... And I, on the other hand, stand in the center of mine. For our universes are not far from each other so that they do not touch; rather, God has pushed them and interwoven them deep within each other.

One of the greatest problems besetting the world today is that across the continents the circles are moving further apart, just at the time when it is imperative that we move closer together so that our realities may once more overlap. Within Christendom I see signs that our circles are coming closer together. But until the circles once more truly merge we belong to a failed church, a still failing church. It was surely not part of Jesus' plan that the church, the body of Christ, should be broken into opposing and inimical factions. And I find it difficult to believe that condemning others as being incapable of reflecting the message of the Gospels because they belong to the wrong denomination is in any way Christian. What about the story of the Lord Jesus who asked water of the Samaritan woman at the well, or who ate with tax collectors, or who drove seven demons from Mary of Magdala?

One of the sorry results of this brokenness is a loss of understanding that the Trinitarian God we profess is indeed the God who is One, the God who is all. I am shocked at the number of people who seem to think that the second person of the Trinity didn't appear until Jesus was born in Bethlehem, or that the Holy Spirit never existed before Pentecost. Surely those who accuse us of polytheism are right unless we believe that the Trinity has always been whole, the Spirit moving over the waters in the beginning, as the Word shouted out the galaxies and the ancient harmonies. This fragmenting of the Trinity is reflected in the fragmenting of our own personalities, our fear of our subconscious minds, our intuitive selves. We are crying out with fear against healing with our extolling of youth and our limiting of love to the merely physical. Physical love is a great joy when expressed in a healthy way, but it is far from being the only kind of love.

Despite all the visible signs of brokenness, all the sharp edges, healing is going on today with something of the same radiance as when Jesus brought Jairus' daughter to life, or gave sight to the blind man on the road to Jericho, or drove demons from a pain-wracked body. It is my hilarious joy to be so clumsy that not only do I fall over furniture, but stumble into and knock down denominational barriers, shoved into them by gracious gusts of the Holy Spirit; and it is a mistake to think that the Holy Spirit is without humour!

I spent a gloriously happy week at the Baptist Bethel Seminary in Minnesota; I have a second home at Mundelein College, where I stay with the Roman Catholic sisters and go to Mass with them (something which was not possible when I first knew them), and an equally happy second home at Wheaton College, which is known as "the Harvard of the Evangelicals." I have spent happy weekends with the Presbyterians . . . oh, and so on. But nowhere have I attempted to alter my own voice, to accommodate, to try to speak in a foreign language. Our circles overlap closely; we discover to our mutual pleasure that we are far closer than we realized, and that many of the harsh arguments going on around us are about peripheral things. And so, through the gift of grace, we are given glimpses of that which is really real.

Reality is not something we observe; something *out there,* as some people used to think that God was something out there. Reality is something we participate in making, as co-creators with God. Making reality is part of our vocation, and one of the chief concerns of prayer. And it is an affirmation of interdependence.

When I turn to the piano and a Bach fugue, I compose it along with Bach as I hear it and attempt to play it. A writer, alone and with great struggle, writes a book. That book becomes real only as someone reads it and creates it along with the author. Each one of us, reading Genesis, will begin to create a new reality. The important thing is that our realities intersect and overlap.

One way of overlapping is to identify with someone else, for instance, in intercessory prayer. To have compassion (com = with; passion = suffering) means to share with another whatever it is that circumstances are bringing to bear on that other. It does not mean to coerce or to manipulate or to dictate ("Of *course* you must sell your house first thing. After that there is nothing for you to do but leave him. What you *really* need is a new wardrobe."); when we coerce or manipulate or dictate we don't have to be involved with the one we are hoping to help. Compassion means to be with, to share, to overlap, no matter how difficult or painful it may be.

And compassion is indeed painful, for it means to share in the suffering of those we pray for; to love is to be vulnerable, and to be vulnerable is to be hurt, inevitably, yet without vulnerability we are not alive, and God showed us this when he came to live with us, in utter vulnerability, as Jesus of Nazareth.

Preparation for this kind of sharing comes with story. When I identify with Adam or Eve, with Cain or Abel, with Abraham or Sarah, this is practice in identifying with all the people around me, in helping our circles overlap. And it is sometimes practice in recognizing the dark side of myself, the side I would rather not acknowledge. Until I can bring myself to acknowledge it, I cannot offer it to God to be redeemed.

If I am both Adam and Eve, so also am I Cain and Abel. Parables and fairy tales make much of older and younger sons. Joseph, for instance, is a younger brother whose ill-advised bragging deserved the animosity of his elder siblings. And Gideon is a younger brother, who by his humble obedience, succeeded in rescuing the exiled Hebrews from their powerful enemies.

We're a mixed lot, but what a rich mix we are, and what material we provide for story—story which gives us glimpses of truth which otherwise might remain hidden!

The First Death

6

ABOUT A DECADE AGO I tried to work out my identification with Cain by writing another story:

The Wages of Innocence

If one has had an unhappy childhood, then all of the naughty acts one commits during adolescence and young adulthood, or even later, are explained, understood, and condoned: forgiveness doesn't really come into it, at least not for me, because I have no idea what it means, or even if I am forgiveable.

My childhood was, in any event, odd. I'm not sure whether it was happy or unhappy, because those were new concepts in our world. My brother and I played from dawn to dark. Sometimes we helped our parents, he more than I. He was the younger of the two of us boys, and I think it made him feel big and important to be told he was a help. If our mother was annoyed with our father, she would praise my brother all the more for any little thing he did for her, so he began to get the idea he was better than anybody.

Our parents, I am sure, are largely responsible for what I did. Ought not parents to shoulder the blame for their children's acts? Our mother and father quarrelled constantly, each one blaming the other for our present low estate. Since my brother and I might very well not have been born in their other estate (though nobody is quite sure about this), they frequently shouted at or hit us because we reminded them that they had known better days. In cold weather my brother's nose ran constantly, and our mother would wipe it distastefully and tell us that in the old days it had never been cold and had rained only at night. There had been enough to eat and to spare, and they didn't have to worry about clothes and nobody knew the difference between work and play and the giants didn't come lumbering around to steal dinner just as it was ready.

When my brother and I were very little we liked the giants and the odd winged creatures who weren't men, being immortal. We, they told us, were mortal, but nobody yet knew what being mortal meant. The giants, like us, were mortal, but they lived in a different chronology, or so we were told, and their life span was longer than ours. What was a life span? We did not know. Some of the giants had only one eye in the middle of the forehead, and six fingers on each hand. They were gentle with small things, and would play games with my brother and me, tossing us back and forth like living balls, and we would squeal with excitement and pleasure. Of course our parents had forbidden us to play with the giants for fear they would harm us, if only by accident, but they never did. With large things they were not so gentle, and we saw them kill dragons and dinosaurs with one blow, though we did not at first know what it meant, to kill. The dragons and the dinosaurs would fall over and twitch and then stop moving and sometimes their blood would come out of them.

The giants told us that this was mortality, but one of the winged men told us not to pay any attention because we, being human, were neither like the giants nor like the dragons and dinosaurs, nor like the beasts of the field.

One particular winged creature took a special interest in us and taught us a great deal. He seemed to be the leader of the others, because they all deferred to him. First of all he showed us how wise it was not to tell everything to our parents; if they didn't know we had been playing with the giants, for instance, they couldn't scold us.

This special winged one was tall, not as tall as the giants but taller than our father, with great dark wings which he could spread like a cloud so that they covered the sun. Once, as he was thus hiding the sunlight, he told us that we must be particularly careful not to tell our parents when we had seen him. "They do not understand me," he said, sadly. "They blame me for what should have been a blessing. *I* was certainly bored in that Garden."

My brother could not keep his mouth closed. While we were eating our pottage that evening he let slip to our parents what the winged one had said.

"That snake! That serpent!" my mother hissed furiously, putting her arms around both of us and pulling us close to her. "Trying to seduce innocent children. Stay away from him, that evil one! If you go near him again I'll have your father beat the living daylights out of you."

I knocked my brother around a bit at bedtime, not to hurt him, you understand, just to teach him to keep his mouth closed next time.

When I saw the winged man again I could see why my

mother called him a serpent. His shape seemed to be changing until now there was something sinuous about it that was
unlike our bodies, a rippling and a darkness that was no
longer shining. "Why does my mother hate you?" I asked
him.

"Hate," he mused, smiling. "It's only the other side of
love."

I tossed this aside. "Yes, but what does she blame you
for? Were you in the Garden when they were there?"

He nodded, stretching his wings and then folding them
in much the same way that I stretched my arms above my
head when I got up in the morning. "Oh, long before they
were there. I can go back any time I want to," he added,
"though I don't want to very often. Dull place. They don't
know when they're well off, your parents."

"Why can you go back if they can't? What about the
cherubim with the flaming sword?"

"Only man was thrown out of the garden," he said. "It's
different for me. I threw myself out, so it's still open to me
and my friends." He indicated some of the other winged
creatures. He grinned. "I've been thrown out of better
places than that."

At this point my brother came leaping up behind us and
scared me half out of my wits. He was like that, full of jokes
and surprises and roarings of laughter. He laughed at all
kinds of things that weren't funny to me at all. Once when
we were kneeling by a still pond to drink and saw our faces
reflected in the water, he threw a pebble at our watching
faces, and laughed and laughed as our expressions changed
and rippled in the moving of the water. He used to sing,
too, and whistle, enough to deafen you, and run and leap
and prance.

My father would shout, "Can't you keep still for a min-
ute?"

My mother would answer him, "Let the child be happy if he can."

My mother used to sing, too, but it was a different kind of singing from my brother's. It was a tuneless humming, and usually came when she was annoyed with my father, or with the Lord El, or with herself, and we learned early that it meant that she was telling us, "*I* don't care. *I'm* all right. I don't need you. Go away."

When the humming went on for too long I would leave the home fire and go. Sometimes my brother would come running after me. "She doesn't mean it. She *does* need us. She really doesn't want you to go."

"You're too young to understand." I told him out of the darkness into which her humming had pushed me.

"Come on home. She's cooking dinner. Father brought home a mammoth and she's broiling mammoth steaks and they smell marvellous."

That was my brother for you: he accepted anything our parents said or did. Mammoths, like the dinosaurs and the dragons which the giants killed, were mortal.

What was mortal? I did not understand, so I asked the great winged one.

But he did not answer the question. Instead he said, "Your father was given all the animals of the earth and air and water to name, and so he has power over them and may do with them as he will."

Why is he telling me this instead of answering my question? I wondered. But I was interested. "My father named me. Does he have power over me?"

"I'm glad you brought that up," the winged one said. "It is significant that this realization should come to you at this point when you are going through a crisis of your identity."

My mind was on power. "Who named my father?"

"The One who shut him out of the Garden."

"So the One has power over my father?" I thought about this for a moment. Then I asked, "Who named you? What is your name?"

The winged one spread out his great leather pinions, darkening the sky so that a few confused drops of rain spattered on the ground at our feet. "I have no name. I am No-Name."

Why did this frighten me? "Then if you have no name—"

He folded his wings calmly and smiled at me. "Then I am Not. And no one has power over me."

"I don't understand." How could he Not Be? There he was, standing right in front of me, larger than life—oh, he was taller than my father by far.

"Why don't you go hunting with your father?" he asked, as though he were answering all my questions. "You're old enough now. It would be a significant experience. You might learn a great deal."

"About what?"

"Not-ness." He laughed. His laugh was not like my brother's laugh. It was more like my mother's humming.

I went back to the home fire. My mother was there, stirring something in a clay pot, and she was singing instead of humming. Her singing was as different from my brother's singing as was her humming. My mother's singing came usually when she was preparing something for us, a special meal, or a new skin coat for cold days. I remembered her singing most when my brother and I were very little and she would hold us in her arms and sing and then kiss us as she put us down on our beds of skin for the night. She sang when she was holding us together in the circle of her song: herself, my father, my brother, and me: not pushing us away. She sang when she had forgotten the Garden.

"No," my brother said. "She has not forgotten it. When she sings she is still there."

"What nonsense," I said, "with that ferocious cherubim at the gates keeping us out, all she talks about is *not* being there."

Our father talked less than our mother about the Garden and the old days. Perhaps it was because he had less time. Food which had been theirs for the taking he now had to sweat for, struggling with thorns and thistles, drought and rain. Unlike our mother he seldom complained. Perhaps he didn't have time for complaints, either. Sometimes in the evenings he would play with my brother and me. Once when we were very small he woke us up and took us to see the night sky. Because we slept from sundown to sunup, we had never seen darkness before, and we were awed and frightened. The sky was hidden behind a black covering, which was filled with thousands of little holes through which the light shone.

"No," my father told us. "They are not holes, my sons, they are stars, and the Lord God knows them all by name as I know the animals, and as I know you."

"Does the Lord have power over the stars, then?" I asked. I was frightened. I thought perhaps the Lord God might decide to throw one of the stars at us if we angered him.

"Who is the Lord God?" my brother asked.

Here at least I could show him that I knew more than he did. "Idiot. The Lord God is the one who threw our mother and father out of the Garden and put the ugly cherubim there to keep everybody out." Then I remembered winged NoName. "Almost everybody, that is." Was it because he had no name that he could go past the flaming sword and into the Garden?

95

"Is the Lord God bad, then?" my brother asked.

"No," our father said. "The Lord God is not bad. But he is not to be understood."

"But if he made you leave the Garden then why isn't he bad?"

Our father stood looking up at the night sky, and at the flaming lights called stars. "God made the night and the day; he made the sun and the moon and the stars. Look at the sky, my sons, and ask yourself if the one who made the stars can be bad."

—Why not? I thought. The stars frightened me.

But my brother gave his pleased and happy laugh. "I see! The Lord God is Good. And he is not to be understood."

After that night my father included us when he made offerings to the Lord God.

"Why do you make the offerings?" I asked.

"In gratitude."

"For being thrown out of the Garden?"

"For food and sleep. For rain and sun. For you, my beloved children."

"And what else?"

"For forgiveness."

"But how can you forgive the Lord God when he threw you out of the garden?"

"No, no," my father said. "I ask him to forgive me."

I went to winged NoName for explanation and instruction. He sat down on a rock and drew me to him, unfolding his wings just enough to protect me from the east wind which had risen, bringing with it a stinging of sand from the desert. "I'm glad you've come to me for further orientation," he said. "Your father is, of course, old-fashioned in his dwelling on guilt. It's morbid, and morbidity is unhealthy.

In the first place, he didn't do anything wrong—"

"But what did he do?" I interrupted. "They've never told me."

"They ate an apple," NoName said. "That's all."

All I knew about apples was that my mother wouldn't let us eat them, and my father got angry when we teased.

"And then," NoName continued, "they learned the difference between good and evil, and so they became a threat to the powers that be, and had to be got rid of."

The difference between good and evil? My mother had called the winged NoName the evil one. To me he was the question-answerer. Perhaps it is evil to answer too many questions?

"You must understand," NoName said, "that your father belongs to the older generation and his attitudes are no longer relevant. What you must do is establish a meaningful relationship with this world. I must go now, but come see me again soon. I enjoy our dialogs."

As we grew older, my brother and I, we had less time to run about and play. We had to help our parents. Our father took us hunting with him occasionally, but mostly he set my brother to keeping the sheep, and me to tilling the ground, because I was older and stronger. Superior. I still went to see NoName whenever I had the opportunity. My brother seldom went with me. Instead, he often used to talk to the horrible cherubim with the flaming sword. And he got into the habit of talking with the Lord.

"But the Lord doesn't answer your questions," I said, "and NoName answers mine."

My brother laughed. "The Lord answers my questions. The sun rising in the morning is an answer. The stars at night are an answer."

I tried to talk to the Lord God, too, but I found it quite

hopeless. First of all I tried to establish a dynamic relationship, like the one I had with NoName. I introduced myself, and then I asked, "What is your name?"

At that moment a storm started to blow up and there was a tremendous crash of thunder, so loud that it silenced the birds. In this thundering silence the Lord God said, "I will be that I will be."

This didn't make any sense, and I wasn't sure I'd really heard him because of the strange silence, so I asked again, "Yes, but do you have a name?"

"I am."

This was as confusing as NoName saying he was Not, and I certainly didn't regard it as an answer. It also made me think of my identity crisis, so I asked him. "Who am I?"

And the Lord God said, "Certainly I will be with thee."

I gave up and started to go. Old-fashioned language confused me. He called after me, "Where is your brother?"

I shrugged. "I should know? He's always hanging around you. You see more of him than I do."

The rain started then, so I left. I was glad of the rain. The ground was dry, and we needed it for the grain.

The next time we made our offerings my brother brought his best lamb, and I brought some of the fruit of the ground that was a bit wilted. As usual, they started talking, the Lord God and my brother. I might not have been there.

"Oh, Lord, my Lord," my brother said, "my heart is ready, my heart is ready, blessed be your Name from the rising of the sun unto the going down of the same. Who is like unto the Lord God who humbleth himself to behold the things that are in heaven, and in the earth!" It was like singing, the way my brother spoke.

"How can he bless your name," I asked the Lord God, "if he doesn't know what it is?" At least NoName had No-

Name, I thought, and didn't play tricks like saying *I will be that I will be.*

As usual the Lord God gave an answer which wasn't an answer: "The earth is given daylight by the fire of the sun, but neither can you look directly at the brightness of the sun without dark coming to your eyes, nor can you understand it; nevertheless it is by the sun that you see."

I left them and went to seek NoName and some proper answers.

NoName was waiting for me by a large rock, and he opened and lowered his leather wings in greeting.

"This Name person," I said, "pays more attention to my brother than to me."

"He's just copying your parents," NoName said. "Too much is demanded of the first child. And yet you are not appreciated nor understood. No wonder you are an under-achiever. Just because your brother has a pretty face and a nice voice is no reason for discrimination. They should try to have a deeper involvement in your self-fulfillment, and help you to realize your potentialities. Now, if your brother were out of the way, of course, things would be different. As long as he's under foot you are going to suffer trauma and distress."

I went to find my brother. He was holding a new born lamb in his arms and he paid more attention to the lamb than he did to me. So I took a stick and hit him with it the way the giants hit the dinosaurs and the dragons.

Still holding the lamb, he fell, and red blood came from his head. I looked at him, and then I told him to get up. But he did not move.

"Get up," I repeated. "You are not a dinosaur or a dragon. NoName said we were different. Come on. Get up."

Still he did not move.

I knelt down beside him. The lamb began bleating and I

pulled it out of my brother's arms and pushed it away. "Get up!" I shouted in his ear. He did not stir. Then I saw that there was no breath in his nostrils, no rise and fall of his chest. The only motion was the slow stream of blood from his temple. His eyes were open as though they were looking at me, but they were not. They were empty, as though there was no one behind them.

Perhaps we were not, after all, so different from the dinosaurs and the dragons.

NoName stood beside me. "So we witness the first human death."

I continued to kneel beside my brother, beating at his chest to make it rise and fall again. "Is this mortality?"

"Yes," NoName said, "also known as death. You are not to blame. Make this quite clear to your parents. It was not your fault. It was theirs. There is no such thing as corporate guilt. They are the ones who sinned, not you. Remember that. It will be very bad for your personality development if they make you feel guilty."

I was not, at that moment, interested in my personality development. "Can't you make him get up?"

"He is dead." NoName snapped his fingers. "Finis."

I blew into my brother's mouth to try to blow breath back into him. But all that happened was that I lost breath myself. I drew back, panting, and NoName was gone.

I ran away from that place and from my brother. If I stayed away for a while and then returned, perhaps he would be singing to the sheep again.

The Lord God said to me, "Where is your brother?"

I answered, "If you don't know, how should I? Am I my brother's keeper?"

I left his Presence and went back to the home fire and told my parents that something had happened to my brother. They both began to run, run, to the place where the sheep grazed. I ran after them. "Perhaps he's all right now," I panted. "I was told that we, being men, were different from the dragons and the dinosaurs. I didn't know he would fall down and not be able to get up. It is not my fault."

We reached the field and the sheep and my brother lying where I had left him, his blood drying on the grass.

My mother flung herself upon my brother, covering his body with hers, crying to him to get up, to move. "O my son, my son," she cried, "my son, my son."

"I didn't know about death. I didn't know," I said loudly. "I am not guilty. Therefore I am innocent."

My father stood very still. All about him there was a kind of terrifying quietness. I shifted my weight from one foot to the other, but my father did not move.

"I am innocent," I said again.

At last my father spoke, slowly, heavily. "Innocence is not enough. When your mother and I chose to eat of the tree of the knowledge of good and evil, innocence was lost. You were ignorant, perhaps, but not innocent."

"Then it was your fault. It wasn't mine."

"We are responsible for our actions," my father said. "This is what it means to be human. In this we *are* different from the dragons and the dinosaurs."

My mother still covered my brother with her body, crying out to him. My father left me and went to my mother. He knelt beside her and beside my brother. He did not look at me again, or speak to me. It was as though I was not there.

He held my mother, at first gently, then, as she began to scream, roughly.

My father knew my mother. He took my mother away and knew her.

After a time I had a baby brother. They called his name, Seth.

How sweet he was, how tiny, tender, and soft. I did not

remember my other brother that way. But I was not allowed to touch this little one. Every once in a while as we squatted around the fire at dinner, my mother would reach out her hand almost as though she were going to touch me. But then instead she would reach into the bowl of food, or put the baby to her breast. My father was no longer angry; he was, instead, sad, except when the baby laughed. But he said that I was no longer to be trusted. After a while I left them and went off to live my own life away from them. The Lord God set a mark upon me so that no one would kill me for bringing death to the world. And NoName laughed at me and said that now all my questions were answered.

O Lord, my God. I think I could have loved my baby brother.

The God
Who Is
Free

7

As CHAPTER FIVE of the Book of Genesis begins, Adam and Eve have left the Garden; Cain has killed Abel; and Adam and Eve have a third son, Seth. Seth has had a son named Enos, though there is no mention of who Seth's wife is. But there must have been some people around, for the last verse of chapter five reads:

> And to Seth, to him also was born a son, and he called his name Enos; then began men to call upon the name of the Lord.

Not until then? Was it because the memory of Eden was becoming dim, and the easy communion with the Lord who walked in the Garden in the cool of the evening was no longer possible? Was it a longing cry of homesickness? As the Lord had called out when Adam and Eve had eaten of the fruit of the forbidden tree, "Where are you?" in wounded love, so were el's people now beginning to ache from their wounds and to call out to their begetter? Was that the beginning of conscious, verbalized prayer? In the Garden, prayer had been all of life; eating, knowing each other, sleeping, all were part of prayer. So wasn't the Fall the breaking of life into fragments which needed to be put together again by prayer?

Chapter five begins:

> *This is the book of the generations of Adam. In the day that God created man, in the likeness of God made he him, male and female.*

The ancient Hebrew lived in a completely patriarchical society, so this reiterated insistence on male and female as the image of God is all the more extraordinary, and all the more wonderful.

Seth was probably the child who gave Adam and Eve the most pleasure and the least grief, though we do not know a great deal about him, beyond his genealogy. He had a son, Enos, who was important not only because it was after he was born that men (male and female) began to call upon the name of the Lord, but because he was an ancestor of Enoch. Enoch walked with God; that is far more important than that he begat sons and daughters, including Methuselah.

> *Enoch walked with God, and he was not, for God took him.*

God took him. He didn't die, like other people. He walked with God, and God took him, as el later took Elijah the prophet.

In terminology which barely overlaps my own circle, Enoch was raptured.

I sometimes see a bumper sticker which I find disturbing. It reads: IN THE CASE OF THE RAPTURE, THIS CAR WILL BE UNMANNED. That strikes me as being highly irresponsible. I have a vision of a VW bug careening along while the occupants are wafted out through the roof, paying no attention to the other cars on the highway being smashed by their abandoned vehicle.

(When my Anglican priest son-in-law, Alan, first visited my husband's family in Tulsa, my mother-in-law asked him barely before he had time to get in the door, "Alan, do you believe in the Second Coming?" "Yes."

That was only the beginning. Later on that day he and Josephine were taken on a drive around Tulsa. Josephine had visited there a good many times, so the focus of showing off the beautiful city was on Alan. A friend of my sister-in-law was driving, and suddenly she asked, "Alan do you believe that at the Second Coming our feet will have left the ground before Jesus's feet touch down?"

My sister-in-law interjected quickly, "Alan, that's the courthouse over there. I do want you to have a good look at it. Dad spent a lot of time there."

To worry about whose feet are where at the Second Coming strikes me as trivializing the Parousia, and yet the questioner was utterly serious. Another case of circles not overlapping. What appears irrelevant to me was important to her.)

However it happened, Enoch walked with God, and God took him. Already, in chapter five of Genesis, God is trampling on death, telling us that death is not going to have the last word.

And, by the end of chapter five, Noah has been born, and so have Shem, Ham, and Japheth.

———◆◆◆———

Five short chapters, and already this Book of Books has out-done the best sellers: sex, the supernatural, violence, murder, and the strange, almost science-fiction story of Enoch, simply vanishing from the face of the earth; after a full life, of knowing his wife and begetting children, Enoch was taken by God. Perhaps, if we walk with God our sense of wonder is untouched, we retain our joy at being simply who we are, faulted and flawed, but God's. Perhaps if we walk with God, our lives are truly nothing but prayer.

For outrageous imagination, chapter six outdoes chapter five. And yet—is it imagination? (Can we imagine anything which is not real?) In the beginning of chapter six we read:

And it came to pass that the sons of God saw the daughters of men that they were fair, and they took them wives...

Who were these sons of God? One theory is that they were fallen angels, which is why things went from bad to worse with poor, fallen human nature. Another theory is that they were an advanced race from a distant galaxy whose space ship was crippled perhaps, forcing them to land on this backwards planet. In any event, they married with us natives, and that is why we have our Leonardo da Vincis and Shakespeares and Beethovens...

And perhaps... but who knows what really happened? The Bible does not tell us, and thus far we do not know.

And then we read,

There were giants in the earth in those days.

Giants? All folk-lore includes stories of giants. In almost every culture there is some version of the story of *Jack and the Bean Stalk*—Jack, the naughty boy, who ends up out-witting the even naughtier giant.

But is it only folk-lore? What about the outline of the great chalk horse in England, a long, running horse which can only be seen from a distance? Or, even stranger, in Peru there are extraordinary markings which are visible as patterns only from the air. From the ground they appear random, but from the air it is apparent that they are not random at all, nor are they accidental patterns of nature; they are deliberate design. What they mean, and who made them, we do not know, just as we do not know more than a fragment of the complex and sophisticated culture of ancient Peru, a strange country, a frightening country, a country of ghosts and unknowns.

————◆◆————

There were giants in the earth in those days,

says verse 4 of chapter six, and it continues:

When the sons of God came in unto the daughters of men, and they bare children to them, the same became mighty men which were of old, men of renown.

And then, immediately following in verse 5, we read,

And God saw that the wickedness of man was great in the earth, and that every imagination of the thoughts of his heart was only evil.

What happened? What turned the people's hearts to wickedness?

We don't know. Very likely it was the same things which turn people's hearts to wickedness today, discontent with who they were and what they had, so that they were easy prey for the temptations of hubris; selfish pride and greed and envy; boredom, lust, violence—all of which result in other people being treated as things, rather than the wonderful creatures, the children of the Creator which we really are.

So verse 6 goes on to say,

And it repented the Lord that el had made man (male and female) on the earth, and it grieved el in the depths of the heart.

Repent is a word used frequently in connection with the Lord of the Old Testament.

The Greek word for repent is *metanoia,* meaning to turn completely around, to reverse directions. The thing which may seem strange to us today is that the word repent, as used by the ancient Hebrew, referred not only to us creatures, but to the Lord: We have done evil in the sight of the Lord; perhaps if we amend our sinful ways el will repent and take away the harshness of the divine judgment. God, in other words, was as free as we are to have a change of mind.

After David had lusted after and taken Bathsheba, after she had conceived a baby by him, and he had planned that her husband be deliberately killed in battle in order that he might marry her, the baby of this illicit union became ill. While the baby had sickened and lay dying, David put on sack-cloth and ashes and fasted, praying that the child might be spared. But when the baby died, he took off the sack-cloth and ashes and asked for food. And he was asked why he wasn't wearing sack-cloth and ashes and fasting now, now that the child was dead. And he replied: What for? As long as the baby was alive there was a chance that God might repent, change el's mind. But el did not, and the baby was dead, so there was nothing to do but get on with life.

There is considerable contemporary argument about the possibility of God's changing. I was sent a sermon recently in which the preacher (whose name was not included) talked about the inadvisability of believing in a "God who is always changing, and therefore, inevitably, becoming what we want him to be." What's inevitable about that? The God to whom David prayed for the life of his son did not change as David would have wanted. The writer of the sermon said, "I am not sure I can worship a God who gives me what I ask for and who is always changing according to the way in which the world changes." But who is to say that if God chooses to change, he chooses to change in the way in which the world changes? It may be completely the reverse, I do not know whether or not, or how, God changes, only that el will be what el will be, and that is what el wills, not what I will. Perhaps there are people who see God changing according to their own manipulation of him (the masculine pronoun again; it gives me an idea of how I feel about this). Manipulation is idolatry, not faith. My faith tells me that God is utterly trustworthy, and that el's love of us is infinite and unfathomable. As long as the Lord will be what el will be, a living Lord still involved in creating, it is always possible that el will repent, either to forgive us when we are truly sorry for our sins, or to punish us when we are discontented, and often don't even know we are sinning, unless there is a prophet to point it out.

And prophets frequently aren't listened to. The great prophets did not concern themselves overmuch with foretelling the future. Instead, they pointed out to the people that they had turned away from the living Lord and were worshiping false gods (mammon, sex, self-righteousness, holier-than-thou-ness, greed, lust, avarice, destructive criticism, judgmentalism . . .). So, when

God saw that the wickedness of people was great on the earth... it repented the Lord that he had made these creatures, and el said, I will destroy man (male and female) whom I have created from the face of the earth.

But—and why on earth?
  Noah (of all people)

found grace in the eyes of the Lord.

Noah: the first of the great Old Testament heroes. An ordinary man, with wife and children, enjoying the legitimate pleasures of the flesh, and enjoying wine rather too much.

Noah found grace in the eyes of the Lord.

The Lord gave Noah specific directions as to how to build the ark, and as I read these directions, I'm not sure how seaworthy the ark sounds, but that doesn't matter, because the Lord is the Director of the heavens and the earth and the seas. Noah listened to the directions, and he did what the Lord told him to do. That's the first thing the Old Testament heroes have in common: when God spoke to them, they recognized the Lord's voice, and they listened, and they obeyed. They might argue; they might obey reluctantly, but they obeyed.

And here we come to a mighty question: How did Noah, and those to come after him, Abraham and Sarah, Isaac and Rebecca, Jacob and Rachel, how did they know that it was the voice of the Lord they were hearing, and not the voice of the tempter? We human beings have often, with the best will in the world, confused the two.

When the crusaders, believing in the holiness of their cause, slaughtered orthodox Christians in Greece, whose voice did they hear? I have a beautiful Jerusalem cross, but

I would never wear it in Greece, because it is a symbol of the massacre of Christians by Christians.

In our own daily lives, in smaller but nevertheless significant ways, how can we tell whose voice it is we are hearing?

Sometimes we can't, for the tempter is extremely clever, and is a superb mimic. But he always slips. If there is even a touch of any of the temptations offered Jesus after the baptism, then it is not the voice of the Holy Spirit we are hearing. If we are gently patted on the back and told that we have a particularly devout and effective prayer group, if we are complimented, ever so gently, on the depth of our spirituality, if we are set apart, even a little, from the rest of creation, then we can make a reasonable guess as to whose voice we are hearing.

When I ride the subway; when I think of the angry man who swung his plastic bag full of bottles at my old dog and me; when I read about drug pushers and rapists, it is not always easy to see these people as my brothers and sisters; but they are, and if I draw my skirts aside then I am drawing away from part of all that God has created. The hem of Jesus' garment must often have been dirty.

If anyone says, loftily, that so-and-so is not saved because so-and-so is a Roman Catholic—or an Episcopalian or a Seventh-Day Adventist—we are equally setting ourselves apart, and this setting apart is always a sign of the presence of the tempter. If we look down from the heights of our theological sophistication on the enthusiasm of the hymn-singers and alleluia-and-praise-the-Lord shouters, we are setting ourselves apart or, even worse, above—another sign that the tempter is breathing sweetly upon us.

John Wesley was a brilliant preacher, and one day after he had preached a great sermon, he was approached by someone who told him what a magnificent sermon it was.

"Yes, I know," he replied. "The devil has already told me."

It is very disturbing to some people to accept that Satan and the fallen angels speak in tongues. Of course they do. After all, an angel is still an angel, even if fallen. We've all heard of churches which have been visited by the Holy Spirit, where the people have praised the Lord in tongues, where joy has abounded in the loveliest possible way. But, as so often happens, if these gifted people begin to think that they are even slightly more gifted and slightly more saved than the rest of the congregation, then it is no longer the Holy Spirit who is speaking through them, though they may not have noticed the takeover.

Of course Noah was special. I am special. Each one of us is special. It is when we begin to feel *more special than* that the trouble begins.

Noah found grace in the eyes of the Lord. God didn't dwell on that, but told Noah how to build the ark, and then told him to bring all the beasts of the earth and fowls of the air into the ark, by sevens, not by twos, as the old song has it. Building the ark cannot have been easy for Noah. Not only did it call for great physical labour, but it must have evoked the laughter and scorn of his friends and neighbours, who probably thought of him as no more than a doom mongerer.

But as the Lord told Noah it would happen, so did it happen, and water covered the face of the earth, and all life that was not in the ark perished.

When finally, after forty days, the torrents of rain stopped and the sun came out, God set a rainbow in the sky as a covenant between the Creator and el's fragile creatures.

And how fragile we are! The end of chapter nine, from verse 21 on, demonstrates this. Here Noah and his family have been chosen from among all the people of the earth to survive the flood and repopulate the planet. Noah planted a garden and a vineyard, and grew grapes, and made wine, and got drunk, and one of his sons "saw" his father's nakedness, as we euphemistically translate it.

Human, frail, faulted, flawed—out of this sorry clay God produces the people, male and female, who are to do el's will, to be el's image. How strange and wonderful that the image of God is not made from an accumulation of perfection and virtue, but from blundering creatures who nevertheless struggle to listen, and to love.

So the earth was repopulated, and life went on much as usual. People were perhaps no worse, but there's no evidence that they were much better. Shouldn't they have been better, after all that had happened? But they weren't.

And so we come to the story of the Tower of Babel, the reverse story of the great day of Pentecost, which was the redemption of Babel, the great day of Pentecost when once again people understood each other when they spoke.

It was not the building of the tower that was wrong, but the reason for it: hubris, once again. If the tower reached to heaven, the builders reasoned, they would be as God.

And, as always when we fall for this particularly effective temptation of Satan, disaster followed, and the Lord said,

> *Go to, let us confound their language, that they may not understand each other's speech.*

And suddenly the people began to speak in different languages, and they could no longer understand one another. The effects of this fragmentation are frighteningly visible today, among the nations, and (more surprisingly and less excusably) within the church.

Of all the roles my husband has played, one of my very favourites is that of Cardinal Cajetan in John Osgood's play, *Luther*. Cajetan has a long, impassioned speech in which he begs Luther not to leave the church. Among other cogent reasons he gives is that we would no longer have one language if the church were divided into denominations, each speaking the language of a different country. Whereas, if the church stayed together, there was always the *lingua franca* of Latin, understood whether one were in France or Germany or Serbo-Croatia. It would be a sorry fragmenting of the body.

It was either Emerson or Thoreau (from either of them it would have been an extraordinary statement) who said that the worst thing to happen to Western civilization was Luther's leaving the church. This statement, considering who made it, cannot be tossed aside. I'm still thinking about it.

Hugh was fascinated by the rôle of Cajetan, and did a good deal of research into the character of this complex man. It so happened that, during the run of the play, friends of ours went to Rome with their two daughters, who were friends of our children. These little girls had not seen the play, and were probably not aware of Hugh's rôle in it. But one day when they were in Saint Peter's Basilica, the younger of the two girls stopped in front of a statue, pointed, and said, "Look! There's Mr. Franklin!"

The statue was of Cardinal Cajetan.

I have no explanation for this kind of marvellous synchronicity. I simply rejoice when it happens.

And synchronicity weaves and interweaves throughout Scripture.

———◆◆———

After the disaster at Babel there's a long column of genealogy, until we come to the begetting of Abraham, Lot, and Sarah. For simplicity's sake I'm going to call them by their familiar names, though as so often happens in Scripture, part way through their lives their names are changed by God; Abram becomes Abraham, and Sarai becomes Sarah. One of the many reasons I wish I knew Hebrew is the importance of the meaning of names. For instance, the Hebrew for Isaac is Itzak, and Itzak means *laughter* (though Isaac had a singularly unfunny life). But I'm getting ahead of the story.

Abraham and Sarah were old. They'd probably used up their social security benefits. They were candidates for a Retirement Village or an Old People's home—had there been such things. Sarah was long past menopause, and Abraham his equivalent thereof. They had lived a full, if childless life, and surely deserved some peace and quiet in their old age. You would certainly think that they were the last people God would pick as pioneers.

But the Lord from whom Jesus refused to turn away when the Spirit led him into the wilderness to be tempted, doesn't pick the logical people to do the work which needs to be done, and that's one of the most important things to know about God. Each one of us, el's creatures, is going to be asked to do things we don't think we can do, and el is going to expect us to do them.

Perhaps that is the meaning of the strange story of the fig tree which did not give figs to Jesus. Nikos Kazantzakis wrote:

> *I said to the almond tree,*
> *Sister, speak to me of God.*
> *And the almond tree blossomed.*

When God asks us to do something, el expects us to do it, whether we think we can do it or not.

Many great things have been accomplished by people the world didn't think adequate to do them. The pages of history are filled with heroic people who have had epilepsy, club feet, were stutterers, short of stature, blind, one-armed...

In a much less sensational way, I was a tongue-tied, shyness-frozen adolescent and young woman. In any public gathering I backed into a corner and tried to become invisible. When I was first asked to give a talk in front of an audience, I had to hold onto the podium, quite literally, in order to stop my knees from buckling under me. It was only when I realized that my shyness and awkwardness were a form of self-centeredness, and that I, myself (or what I thought of as myself) didn't matter, that I began to be able to open my mouth and speak, to look at the other person's needs instead of my own, to be able to reach out instead of drawing back.

We do occasionally learn from our mistakes. When I am enabled freely to throw my arms around someone in spontaneous pleasure at meeting, I am reminded of an occasion in my young womanhood when I was in my mother's hospital room (she was there for some minor surgery), and a friend of mine came in, to see me, as well as to visit my mother. We hadn't seen each other in a while, and she held out her arms in greeting and I, the Yankee cousin frozen into shyness in the midst of all the southern kin, did not return the gesture, not realizing until later that this reticence could well have been interpreted as rebuff.

It wasn't till long after that experience that the human touch became a joy to me, but the acute awareness that I had not returned love with love was a lesson I will never forget. It was not a lesson I learned that day, once for all. It is a lesson I never stop learning.

Slowly I have realized that I do not have to be qualified to do what I am asked to do, that I just have to go ahead and do it, even if I can't do it as well as I think it ought to be done. This is one of the most liberating lessons of my life.

The qualifications needed for God's work are very different from those of the world. In fact, when we begin to think we are qualified, we have already fallen for the tempter's wiles. Not one of us has to be qualified in order to employ lesson, meditation, and orison; to read, think, and pray over Scripture. We do not need to have gone to a theological seminary, or to have taken courses in Bible in or out of college. We do have to be willing to open ourselves to the power of the living Word. And sometimes that can be frightening.

But we are in good company. Surely Abraham and Sarah were frightened when the Lord said to them.

> *Leave your country, leave your family, and go to a land which I will show you. And I will make from you a great nation, and I will bless you, and make your name great, and you will be a blessing.*

The story of Abraham and Sarah is many-layered, and over the centuries we have barely scratched the surface of all that it means. But we turn back to it, again and again, because it gives us glimpses of the nature of the God who was called *Abba*—Father—by Jesus. God's calling of Abraham and Sarah demanded a response which was not action alone, but action which was prayer.

And God continued,

> *And I will bless them who bless you, and curse them who curse you, and in you shall all families of the earth be blessed.*

All families, not just a few here and there, separated from the rest of the population, but all families of the earth shall be blessed, whether we deserve it or not.

Would we listen if the Lord asked of us what he asked of these old people? I hope we would, but I'm not sure, Nor am I sure that if we listened, and heard, we would have obeyed. But Abraham and Sarah, and Abraham's nephew, Lot, and all their retinue,

went forth to go into the land of Canaan.

All was going well with the journey for these intrepid voyagers, and then there was a famine so severe that Abraham went into Egypt for food. But he was afraid that if he admitted that Sarah was his wife, he might be killed, for Abraham, suddenly looking at Sarah with fresh eyes, said to her,

I'm aware that you are a fair woman to look upon, therefore the Egyptians will kill me, but they will save you and keep you alive.

So he asked Sarah to pretend she was only his sister because, according to the custom of that time and that part of the world, it was all right for a stranger to sleep with a man's sister, but not with his wife. If one of the noble Egyptians looked upon Sarah, and wanted her, and knew that she was Abraham's wife, they would have to kill him first to have her.

Pragmatic, our father Abraham.

So they left Egypt when the famine was over and continued on their way. Abraham's and Lot's servants quarrelled, and because Abraham did not want dissension between himself and his nephew, they agreed to go their separate ways. Lot went to Sodom, where he was taken captive, whereupon his uncle

armed his trained servants, born in his own land, three hundred and eighteen.

to rescue Lot.

Scripture is often specific about numbers. Numbers are their own language, and it has been suggested that if and when we make contact with a culture from another galaxy, we should try to communicate with a binary code using numbers, rather than words. Nevertheless, numbers have their own magic, and musicians, such as Bach, are very aware of the importance of them.

After Abraham had rescued Lot he was blessed by Melchizedek. In spite of the conjectures of theologians and historians, he remains a mysterious figure. He was

a priest of Salem, and also a priest of the most high God.

And the psalmist foretold of Christ that he would be

a priest forever, not in the Aaronic priesthood, but after the order of Melchizedek.

Of course, Melchizedek was a priest long before the Hebrew temple was built, or the ark of God, long before the Lord gave the stone tablets of the commandments to Moses, long before Aaron became high priest, long before the tabernacle and the Holy of Holies. But Melchizedek was a herald of things to come, because he brought bread and wine to Abraham, thereby prefiguring the Eucharist.

Abraham continued the journey after this refreshment, but he was still unhappy because he had no children, and he complained to God about this.

That's another thing the heroes of the Old Testament have in common: whenever they are disturbed or upset they complain to God, loudly and uninhibitedly.

I am often surprised at the number of people who think it is somehow wrong to complain to God. When I complain to God, I don't take it out on my family and friends. And when I complain to God, I am often shown what it is that I am really complaining about, and that I am being silly, or trivial, or selfish, or cowardly. Or that I am in deep trouble and it is right to turn to my Maker. When I vent my feelings on God, el will give me the courage, or other gifts I need that I might very well not have received if I had been too reticent to complain.

Abraham was not afraid to complain. So God took him out one night and said,

Look now toward heaven and tell the stars, if you are able to number them ... so shall your seed be.

What an extraordinary promise to make to an old man! But Abraham

believed in the Lord.

God does not ask us to believe the reasonable things; why should el? Believing in what is reasonable is no problem. El asks us to believe that which is not so much unreasonable as that which exists on the other side of reason. So that all that I base my life on is beyond reason, beyond proof.

Believing is never easy, and it is not cheap. Yet Abraham believed, and he did what the Lord told him to do.

And when the sun was going down, a deep sleep fell upon Abram, and lo, a horror of great darkness fell upon him.

I think that most of us have known something of this horror. *Terror anticus,* it is called. It is part of the price of faith. The greater the jewel we seek, the higher the price. But it is worth it. It is worth it.

In those days, if a woman were childless, she could bear her husband a baby through the body of her maid. It is difficult for us on our overcrowded planet to understand the vital importance of children for the nomadic peoples of those days. Children were a matter of life and death, not only for the individual family, but for the preservation of the tribe, the community. If there were not enough hands to bring in the crops, to protect the tribe from the enemy, disaster would follow.

So Sarah sent her maid, Hagar, in to Abraham, and she conceived, and when she saw that she had succeeded where Sarah had not, she despised the older woman. How bitter that must have been for barren Sarah. So she sent Hagar away, and in due time Hagar bore a son, Ishmael, and Ishmael means *bitterness*.

The story might well have been different if Hagar had not scorned her mistress. But she did, and there are depths below depths in the story of Hagar, and of Ishmael, too. Their story, being part of Abraham's and Sarah's story, was a familiar one to the people of Jesus' time; it was part of their mythic language, which runs in the bloodstream. When the child of the slave was compared to the child of the free woman in Paul's Galatian epistle, there were probably few people who did not remember Hagar's scorn of her mistress. And Hagar, in looking down on Sarah, had fallen into the trap of the tempter, and bitterness followed.

Chapter fifteen begins,

The word of the Lord came to Abraham in a vision.

Scripture is full of visions, and they are to be taken seriously and tested very carefully. It may be appalling to us to accept that Satan can speak in tongues, mimicking the Holy Spirit angelically; so also can he send visions, and all visions must be tested against the temptations in order for us to know who has sent them, and whether or not we can trust them. People have had visions where they were told to murder, and they have obeyed these terrible visions, and the result has been sorrow on earth and in heaven.

Anything good (kything, visions, physical love) is immediately imitated and distorted by the tempter, but that does not make the original good any less good, or change or alter the original good which God made.

When the Lord of heaven and earth sends us a vision it is for a good reason. God often speaks to us at night, when we have let down our defences and are quiet enough to hear his voice. When we try to take control of our lives, and perhaps the lives of some of the people around us, our eyes and ears are closed to God's visions.

Scientists and artists both know that visions and inspiration come when least expected. Often we will worry over a problem, brooding fruitlessly, and when we have let it go, suddenly the answer will be there, just when we have stopped looking for it. Sometimes when I am walking my dog at the end of the day, and my mind and body are tired, I will simply walk without thinking, letting my mind roam free. And then I am often given unexpected and beautiful gifts. And sometimes I am given horrors.

As a story teller I have been trained to think of every possibility that can happen to my characters, and this training seeps off the page into what is happening in my own life, and the lives of my family and friends. And so, as I can imagine all the good things, so can I imagine the terrible.

And, if I am open to the good things, I am also, as a consequence, open to the bad.

In *The Time Trilogy* there are evil creatures called the *echthroi*. The singular is *echthros,* a Greek word which simply means *the enemy.* It is an enemy-sounding word, and I have come to understand that the enemy rejoices whenever I project a fearful vision. If someone is late driving home, I have immediate visions of all kinds of terrible accidents, and there have been enough accidents in our lives so that I know that they do happen. But I try to shut off each bad projection, superimposing a lovely one instead. If there is too much talk of nuclear warfare, again I pray for the planet by visualizing it as whole and beautiful, perhaps in the autumn, when gold and scarlet sweep across the landscape. Or I visualize my family during a time of happiness, a festival dinner, with all the candles lit, and all of us holding hands around the table.

If the ugly visions persist, "Lord!" I cry, "Protect me from echthroid projections!" And, "Send your holy angels to cleanse me, mind, body, spirit. Send your angels to banish the echthroi." And I say the prayer from the office of Compline:

> Visit this place, O Lord, and drive far from it all snares of the enemy; let your holy angels dwell with us to preserve us in peace; and let your blessing be upon us always; through Jesus Christ our Lord. Amen.

And I sing the ancient monastic hymn:

> *From all ill dreams defend our eyes,*
> *From nightly fears and fantasies.*
> *Tread under foot the ghostly foe*
> *That no pollution we may know.*

Some of these words seem even more applicable now than they did when they were written, centuries ago. No pollution? How do we escape the pollution of greed, and lust for power, and hardness of heart? And the more modern pollutions of noise and filth and contaminated air and water?

However, if I am totally immune from the projections of the ecthroi, from the horror of great darkness, from terror anticus, then I immunize myself also from the visions which the Lord sends. And I must trust the Lord and el's angels to guard and protect me.

Rainer Maria Rilke said that he was afraid that if he vanquished his demons, his angels would leave him, too. So here we are, once again caught in paradox. And we often refuse to accept the paradox by calling visions unreal, figments of the imagination, delirium, madness, hysteria. We don't want to let go our control.

So it is not surprising that it is during sleep ("Samuel! Samuel!") that our manipulative selves let go their rigid authoritarianism, and our dreams come to us, with messages sometimes quiet and beautiful, sometimes terrible, so that we wake up, trembling. Most of us have recurring dreams. I go, periodically, to a beautiful house, a house I have never been to, but whose many rooms are well known to me, and whose beautiful views rest the troubled spirit.

Then there is the waking dream. I hope I never outgrow my need for daydreams, for they are a part of the healthy psyche—as long as we do not confuse them with reality.

———◆◆◆———

Far different is the relaxing control which comes as a gift. It is the goal of contemplation, and although it can be sought consciously, it cannot be attained consciously. When it happens it is given to us. And sometimes it is given to us in surprising ways and in surprising places and when we are not even looking for it.

One Sunday in July each summer, Hugh and I take the worship service for the Congregational church in the village, and to be asked to do this, and to do it, is a special privilege. Our two younger children were baptized in this church. I have cried, laughed, learned, questioned in this church. To work on a sermon to be preached from the old wooden lectern is probably a more demanding task than to prepare one to be preached from the great stone pulpit of the Cathedral in New York.

Last summer after the church service I said to Hugh, "Go on and get the paper. I want to walk home down the lane." We were having friends in for dinner and I wanted to pick wild flowers.

It was a perfect July day, the sky high and blue with a few fairweather clouds; warm, but not humid, with a gentle, northwesterly breeze. I ambled down the lane, pausing to pick flowers as I saw them, daisies, buttercups, and my mind happily drifted with the breeze. And I was not thinking at all. And then I moved, was moved, into what I suppose would be called an altered state of being. It is, when it happens, a far deeper state of being than the one we live in normally. Everything is more real. The sheer beauty of creation has something of the fresh miraculousness of Eden. Wonder and awareness are heightened. Friendship and love are deeper and richer than anything we encounter in ordinary living, and that is indeed a strong statement, for friendship and love are what make the wheels go round.

When I am returned to myself, as it were, then the glory fades, and once it is over it cannot really be recalled nor described. But it is glory, and it is a way of being that I believe we were meant to know. The loss of it is one of the results of the Fall. These glimpses of reality are not given frequently; we could not often bear such intensity. I suspect that this gift of reality is a gift of the deepest kind of prayer. I know that it cannot be sought consciously, that like all prayer which is out on the other side of words it comes from the infinite grace of God. It is not easily talked about, not only because it is impossible to describe, but because in this frenetic world it is neither easy nor customary to pause and listen to God, and when we talk about people having visions, we're more apt to think they're ready for the mental institution than that they are receiving a message from the Lord.

But we live by revelation. Paul writes in his second letter to the people of Corinth about being taken up to the third heaven, whether in his own body or out of it he is not sure. And immediately after this glorious experience he complains that he has a thorn in the flesh, and that he has asked God not once, but three times, to take it away from him. And the answer is, "No, Paul. My strength is made perfect in your weakness."

Ecstasy is frequently followed by pain, and perhaps it is the joy that gives us the courage to bear the pain, and to experience the pain as birth pain, and to offer our weakness to our Maker, knowing that it can be turned to el's strength.

We were meant to be finely-tuned receivers, but we have created our own static, the messages are no longer clear; we are losing our ability to tune in, an ability we desperately need to renew.

But sometimes the gift is given, as it was as I walked down the old dirt road and my human feet trod glory.

Paradoxes in Prayer

8

AND THE LORD came to Abraham in a vision, saying, Fear not, Abraham. I am your shield and your exceedingly great reward.

And Abraham said, Lord God, what will you give me, seeing I go childless?

And the Lord brought him out and said, Look now toward heaven, and tell the stars, if you are able to count the number of them: and he said, so shall your seed be.

God does not hesitate to repeat something if it is important.

And Abraham believed in the Lord, and el counted it to him for righteousness.

Abraham believed, and Abraham did not believe, because, later on, God spoke to Abraham about his wife, Sarah, and said,

> *I will bless you, and give you a son also of her; yes, I will bless her, and she shall be a mother of nations, kings of people shall come from her.*
>
> *Then Abraham fell upon his face and laughed, and said in his heart, Shall a child be born to him that is a hundred years old? And shall Sarah, who is ninety, bear a child?*
>
> *And God said, Sarah your wife shall bear you a child indeed, and you shall call his name Isaac.*

Isaac. Itzak. Laughter. Where was the joke?

The story flows on. One day Abraham

> *sat in the tent door in the heat of the day, and he lifted up his eyes and looked, and lo, three men stood by him.*

Abraham and his three angelic guests. For the ancient Hebrew an angel was not only a messenger of God, an angel was an aspect of God, was God. So those angels were an icon of the Trinity, the Trinity which was, from the beginning, before the beginning, and will be at the fulfillment of all things.

One of the greatest thrills for me was to see in Saint Basil's Church in Moscow that magnificent icon of Abraham and his three guests. There was the Trinity, sitting at the table, with bread and wine, an affirmation of the dignity of all creation, and the magnificent mystery of the Creator. And the affirmation was all the more poignant because Saint Basil's Church, with its multi-coloured onion domes, like something out of a fairy tale, stands in Red Square, in a state which denies the existence of God. (I did not know until we reached Moscow that *red* and *beautiful* are the same word in Old Russian, and that Red Square was so named in the fifteenth century.)

So I looked at the icon of the Trinity and thought of Sarah, who was summoned from the tent. She, too, is told that she is going to bear a child, and she, too, thinks that the idea is hilarious. It cannot have been happy laughter. Sarah had wanted a baby for a long time, so long that a baby was no longer even a possibility. It must have seemed a cruel joke indeed that now that it was too late, now that she had given Abraham a child by Hagar, her maid, and had been scorned, now, after all these years of hope and disappointment, she is told the incredible—that her withered womb is going to ripen and open and she is going to have a son.

And she does. For man it is impossible; for God, nothing is impossible.

("I didn't laugh," Sarah protested. "Oh, yes, you did," insisted the Lord.)

And so, despite incredulous laughter, Sarah conceives and bears a child, and his name is called Isaac.

God's ways are not our ways. Often we would like them to be our ways. Each generation in turn creates its own god in its own image, thereby hoping to tame all Glory in order to make it comprehensible. It is the attempt to make a poor photocopy of God which produces all the confusion about God's sex, thereby further confounding us about our own sexuality. And we are as confused as were the ancient Romans in the frantic centuries before Rome fell. To bear a child is considered by some people to be degrading (like reading the Morning Office in the bathroom?). Pleasure becomes more important than joy. Transitory thrills are offered as the cure for boredom, restlessness, and that discontent which is surely not divine.

Abraham and Sarah were simpler than we are in many ways, as a nomadic people, close to the rhythms of the earth, dependent on community; one did not make it alone in the desert. There the stars at night were like the stars at sea, undimmed by city lights. They must at times have been overwhelming.

I like my creature comforts, my stove and refrigerator and washing machine, and certainly, oh, most certainly, my electric typewriter, and even the black felt pen I used on the ship as I began to set down these thoughts on the back of the ship's daily newsletter. But technology, for all its obvious advantages, has its limitations, and has dimmed our sense of the numinous. At Crosswicks when the power goes out, as it does in winter ice storms or summer thunder storms, and the rooms are lit only by firelight and candlelight, then the darkness comes alive, as it must have been alive for Abraham and Sarah. Shadows move, stretch up the walls, shrink down again. We cannot quite see what that dark shape is, lurking in the corner. The fear of darkness is supposed to be an acquired fear, but I suspect that we acquire it early, inheriting it from our father, Abraham. The old Scots were totally serious when they included these words in their litany: "From ghoulies and ghosties and things that go bump in the night, the good Lord deliver us."

Abraham and Sarah knew the fear of ghoulies and ghosties and things that go bump in the night (they'd never have denied their existence by banning books which mention them); and they had absolute trust that the good Lord would deliver them, even when they laughed at el's outrageousness. For even when God spoke to them in the form of three angels, el was present, tangibly present, giving el's creatures free will, and then poking a celestial nose in, poking a finger in the pie, being part of the story, which is, after all, God's story.

But if it is el's story, where do we come in? What happens to our free will?

There are many people who believe that we have no free will at all; that everything is predetermined. Each event leads to another, unchangeable event. Ultimately everything will wind down. We will die. The universe will flicker out.

Then, among those who tolerate the thought of free will, there is an increasing tendency to believe that free will dooms us to failure. That when God created us free, free to make wrong choices, as Adam and Eve made wrong choices, el made our failure inevitable.

But why? If we are free to fail, we are also free not to fail. We are free to love God, and to be obedient to el's will. Our free will is most evident when we are being co-creators with God. We may have little free will about outward events, granted. There was nothing most of us could do with our free will to stop the eruption of war in the Falklands. We cannot stop the fighting in the Middle East. Our free will lies only in our response. To be able to respond is to be human, and I learn about this human free will from the great characters in Scripture.

Genesis is a book of contradiction and paradox, just as our lives and thoughts are full of contradiction and paradox. Indeed I am beginning to feel that without contradiction and paradox I cannot get anywhere near that truth which will set me free.

Abraham and Sarah, leaving the comforts of home and going, in their old age, out into the wilderness, were following God's way, definitely not the world's way. In the New Testament it is spelled out even more clearly: we are to be *in* the world, but not *of* it.

In New York, far more than when we are at Crosswicks, we cannot escape being surrounded by the world, and we are constantly offered the world's temptations, sometimes in extreme forms. When someone asked Hugh where the hot new night spots were his response was laughter; the hot night spots are no temptation for us. But there are other, subtler temptations. The more brittle women's libbers (who have lost a view of true liberation) are terrified to accept their fair share of man, made in the image of God, male and female, and abdicate their responsibility by insisting on being their "own woman," and fulfilling their potential by seeking pleasure, or success, or money, at any cost. I am seriously advised that I have really not been fulfilled because I have limited myself to one man, and that any personal problems I may have are the result of this limitation. Or, they may be the result of my parents' overprotectiveness; or, perhaps, their underprotectiveness. If I listen, my free will becomes undermined. Or rather, if I listen without selectivity. Women *are* supposed to be themselves. Her true self is what Jesus made Mary Magdalene when he freed her of possession by seven devils. She became her own woman by completely surrendering herself to the Lord; and it was to Magdalene that Christ first showed himself after the Resurrection.

Keeping myself for one man does not mean that I do not have deep and fruitful friendships with other men. These friendships strengthen rather than lessen, my love for the one man with whom I made my promises. And the same thing which is true for me is true for him.

We *are* supposed to free ourselves from unhealthy ties to our parents, childish overdependencies. But we are not supposed to free ourselves from genuine love and concern.

Pleasure in itself is not a bad thing; it is a good thing. But when we seek it frantically, we lose it. One of my favourite pleasures is soaking my weary bones in a hot bath. It is particularly a pleasure because when our children were very young, and we were living in Crosswicks year round, running the general store in the village, we didn't have enough money to pay for the oil to heat the water for regular tubs for the entire family. So about twice a week I would fill the tub and put one of the children in with me. As soon as we could afford private baths, it occurred to my children that this was one time when they could be with me alone, and frequently one of my daughters would ask, "Mother, can I come talk to you while you take your bath?" And now my grandchildren do the same thing. So when I get into a hot bath, all by myself, it is a privilege, and one I have never yet taken for granted. And it is all the more special because it has not always been my privilege. It is, I trust, an innocent pleasure, but it is surely a pleasure.

It reminds me of a young woman I met at a writers' conference. She was a successful writer for magazines all across the country, and was leading the nonfiction workshop. In awe and amazement, the second day of the conference, she said, "Last night was the first night I have ever spent in a room all by myself." She had slept in a room with her sister until she was married, and ever since then in a room with her husband, whose work did not take him away from home. To spend a night all by yourself for the first time! What a pleasure! So is ice cold lemonade on a hot day, or running across the sand into the water, or curling up under the eiderdown on a cold night.

Seeking pleasure as the ultimate good, however, leads to all the porno houses on Times Square in New York, which once was the glamorous Great White Way of the theater, but which is now ugly and shoddy. The pursuit of pleasure when pushed to the present extremes leads to perversion and violence. Instead of affirming the dignity of human beings, pleasure misused turns us into things to be used and tossed away.

Abraham and Sarah had no time for this kind of pleasure, nor did our forbears. Staying alive took all the energy the human creature possessed. The people who built our home, Crosswicks, around two hundred twenty-five years ago, worked from morning to night. The great beams of the house were hewn from forests of virgin pine. About four miles from the house is the last stand of the old trees left in the state, and it makes me understand Longfellow's lines:

This is the forest primaeval,
The towering pines and the hemlocks.

Both men and women were essential to survival. Candles had to be made; meals cooked, wool spun, meat salted. Simply living was a full-time job. Pleasures did not have to be frenetically looked for; an evening of singing and dancing for the entire community brought great joy.

Let me not sentimentalize our forbears, for they were human beings, as pragmatic as Abraham passing Sarah off as his sister, as shaken by terror of great darkness, as stubborn and self-centered as the men and women of Scripture. But perhaps they were blessed in not having time for massage parlors and adult bookstores and nervous breakdowns, nor time to spend on worrying about self-fulfillment and all the other self-indulgences which come with too much spare time; we all need some time for ourselves, some quiet be-ing time, but too much time, like too much of anything brings trouble.

The paradox is that self-surrender instead of being a denial of personal pleasure brings with it the gift of joy which is to be found in true pleasure. Sarah had to let go her bitter laughter and surrender herself before she could conceive Isaac and receive God's gift of true laughter.

But paradox and contradiction were no surprise to Abraham and Sarah. They were not surprised to see angels, even though they laughed at their messages. They knew how to get themselves out of the way in order to listen. What we call contemplative prayer was an ordinary and essential part of their lives.

In the Western world in the past several centuries we have denied ourselves this kind of total communion with the Creator because we have been afraid of it. Not just we, as individuals, but we in the corporate body of the church, where the tendency has been to sweep the numinous under the rug and pretend it isn't there. Many students ask me about Zen methods of contemplation, about Hinduism, about Sufi, and are astonished to hear that we Christians have a heritage of contemplative prayer without our own scriptural tradition.

The methods of contemplative prayer are similar in all traditions. Sit quietly, preferably comfortably, so that your body works for you, rather than against you. The fourteenth century mystic, Richard Rolle, said that he liked best to sit, "because I knew that I longer lasted... than going, or standing, or kneeling. For... sitting I am most at rest, and my heart most upward."

One of my most-loved places for this kind of prayer is a large glacial rock on which I stretch out, flat on my back, so that I can feel that I am part of the turning of the planet, so that rock and I merge, becoming part of the energy of creation.

Having found the physical context, breathe slowly, rhythmically, deeply. Fit the words of your mantra to this rhythm. And don't be afraid of the word, *mantra*. One young college student came to me full of self-righteous indignation, saying that the use of a mantra was forbidden in the Bible.

"Where?" I asked.

She did not know. But it was there.

Jesus warned us against *vain* repetition. But allowing the name of Jesus to be part of our life rhythm is never vain unless we try to take credit for it.

"But the Bible says a mantra..."

"*Please* go home and check the Bible and see if you can find out where it is forbidden, and come back and bring me chapter and verse," I suggested.

If she looked it up, she didn't find it, not in a concordance, not in the text.

Mantra is simply a convenient borrowed word for the kind of prayer that is constant, which helps us to pray at all times—which the Bible *does* tell us to do. For the Christian, the mantra can be any short petition from the Bible, preferably one which includes the name of Jesus. The most frequently used petition is the cry of the blind man on the road to Jericho, *Lord Jesus Christ, Son of the Living God, have mercy on me, a sinner,* or the shorter version, *Lord Jesus Christ, have mercy on me.*

This is familiarly known as the Jesus Prayer, and I am uncomfortable whenever anyone says, "I use the Jesus Prayer," for we never "use" the Jesus Prayer. It uses us.

And far too often we take the name of Jesus casually, or, even worse, possessively. I do not want to be what my husband calls "a bumper-sticker Christian." Recently we were parked behind a car with two bumper stickers. The one on the left said I LOVE MY PEKINGESE. The one on the right said I LOVE JESUS. Somehow I do not put much stock in that kind of love! Perhaps I was turned off by I LOVE MY PEKINGESE and I LOVE JESUS side by side because there was something possessive about those messages, something separating the owner from those who have neither pekingese nor Jesus as pets. That scares me. The Word is not a pet. The Word is the wildness behind creation, the terror of a black hole, the atomic violence of burning hydrogen within a sun. (Christ is both lion and lamb, and lions are not domesticated.)

A minister friend of mine in the midwest was parked beside a car, at a red light, and the other car had the familiar bumper sticker HONK IF YOU LOVE JESUS. The car behind them began to honk insistently, and the man in the car with the bumper sticker got out, went to the honking car, leaned in the window and said, "You goddam fool, can't you see there's a red light?"

The man who had been honking replied mildly, "But I just love Jesus!"

Remember what Jesus had to say about someone who called his brother a fool?

A friend of mine, an old and holy man, occasionally talked about people he felt were "bejeezly." The people in the above two stories were bejeezly, using the name of Jesus trivially, thoughtlessly, smugly. Anyone saying the Jesus Prayer with such an attitude is tampering with the incredible Power of the Word which created all things. We must approach the name of Jesus humbly, in the same way that we approach the table to receive the bread and wine.

"But doesn't the Jesus Prayer seem selfish?" I am sometimes asked. "Isn't it selfish to ask it for *me?*"

We must learn that we never ask it for ourselves alone. *Me* is always the Body. And when I am praying for someone, holding onto the Jesus Prayer, *me* is whoever I am praying for.

When I was given this prayer by my spiritual director two decades ago, I, too, asked if it wasn't selfish, and he didn't even bother to answer my question, knowing that the Jesus Prayer itself would inform me. And it did. When we have been with this prayer long enough it becomes part of our life rhythm. When I wake up at night it comes bubbling up into my conscious mind like a little fountain—somewhat like the fountain in the wilderness which the Lord made to spring up for Ishmael. When I am frightened or in pain I hold onto it like a drowning sailor holding onto a rope. When I was going under anesthesia for some scary surgery (well, all surgery is scary) I held tightly to the life line of the Jesus Prayer, and there it was, holding me up out of the deep waters as I came back to consciousness.

A friend of mine who had a frightening series of episodes where her heartbeat raced alarmingly, clutched at the Jesus Prayer to calm her panic, *and* her heart beat, and then wondered if it was all right to say such a prayer in order to slow down the out-of-control rhythm of her heart, for the Jesus Prayer did indeed alleviate the wild acceleration. And I could only say that God wants us to be healthy, and that she was not "using" the Jesus Prayer, but holding onto it faithfully, so that she could offer herself to God and allow her body to respond according to el's will.

I do not understand the radiant power of the Jesus Prayer, but I am grateful for it every day. And perhaps it is just as well not to understand, because if we did, we might indeed be tempted to "use" it, to treat it merely as a tool.

One time, more than thirty years ago, after I had come very close to death, I had a terrible dream which recurred to haunt me for a good many years. I would wake up from it in a cold sweat of terror. There were various settings for the dream, but the constant element was that I could not light the lamps in whatever room I was in. I would reach for a light switch, or a lamp pull, and the light would not come on. It would not come on because there was evil in the room, keeping it in darkness. It was the evil which was so terrible, and I would rush frantically from light to light, but the light was under the power of the evil. Sometimes I knew where the evil was, coiled like a snake, and I could not pass it. One time when I was visiting my mother in the South, it was in the hall between her room and mine, coiled around a small bookcase which held a set of encyclopaedias, and it would not let me by to get to my mother. Another time it was in our apartment in New York, possessing the kitchen. The setting varied, but the terror was the same, and I would wake up from the dream cold with terror. It was Abraham's horror of great darkness in its most extreme form.

One night, after I had been given the Jesus Prayer, and it had been deep within me for quite some time, I dreamed this dream again. This time the setting was a house in London. I was in a room on the top floor, and as usual in the dream I was rushing from lamp to lamp, but the evil had control of the light. The evil was coiled across the door sill, so that I could not get out of the room to get down the stairs, and the evil possessed the stairs. And then, suddenly, in the dream, I was holding onto the Jesus Prayer, and the strong rope of this prayer took me through the miasma of evil, all the way down the stairs, and out into the brilliant sunlight.

I have not had the dream since, and that is twenty years. I may have it again; I do not know. But I do know that the evil cannot permanently quench the light, that the light shines in the darkness, and that it will be there for me, bright and beautiful, forever.

I do not always say the Jesus Prayer well, but that is all right; it helps me, not the other way around. And it has helped to show me the aim of contemplative prayer.

The aim of the oriental method of contemplative prayer is total loss of self—nirvana. My son-in-law, Alan, tells me that *nirvana* means "where there is no wind." For the Christian the wind of the Spirit is all-important, that Spirit which brooded on the face of the waters in the beginning, which spoke through the prophets, and which came to us as our Comforter after the Ascension. We do not seek to go to that place where there is no wind, where there is nothing.

Rather than the total loss of self which comes with nirvana, the aim of the Christian contemplative is discovery, our discovery of God and by God. We seek God not in order to find but to be found. When God discovers me in the deepest depths then I am truly Named, and rather than ceasing to be, I *become*.

It is a meeting of lovers.

John of the Cross wrote:

Let us rejoice, beloved,
And let us go forth
To behold ourselves in your beauty,

And he wrote again:

... that I may resemble you in your beauty, and you resemble me in your beauty, and my beauty may be your beauty, and your beauty my beauty; wherefore I shall be you in your beauty, and you will be me in your beauty, because your beauty will be my beauty; and therefore we shall behold each other in your beauty (Spiritual Canticle, *stanza 36, no. 5*).

It *is* a mountain-top experience (as the cliché has it), but we must remember that for one Mount of Transfiguration there were multiplied days of fishing, ploughing the fields, walking the dusty roads. The daily duties must be done before we are given a glimpse of glory. As an old southern woman said, "I don't mind cookin', 'cept hits just so damn daily."

We can get hooked on too many mountain-top experiences, and this is as dangerous as drugs. Our love of God, and God's love for us, is most often expressed in dailiness.

The incarnation is an affirmation of the value and richness of dailiness, and of the rhythm of work and play.

We get out of rhythm, out of synchronization, and a Quiet Day, a retreat, a place and time apart from the regular round of dailiness can help us to reestablish the rhythm.

My annual birthday present to myself is a retreat at the convent of the Community of the Holy Spirit, just a few blocks from our apartment—but it might be half way around the world. I move into silence slowly, but also with a feeling of homecoming. The Sisters still eat in silence, except on special days, and since they are a teaching order, the silence must be a welcome relief. During the day most of the Sisters are teaching at school, and I can be in the chapel by myself (but never alone), or in the peace and privacy of my room. In the early morning, at noon and in the late afternoon and evening, I share in the Offices. I am nourished in all areas of myself, and then am better able to return to the dailiness of the ordinary working day.

Simone Weil writes, "The key to the Christian concept of studies is the realization that prayer consists of attention. It is the orientation of all the attention of which the soul is capable towards God."

(Orientation: "Eastward-ness." Fascinating.)

"The quality of the attention counts for much in the quality of the prayer. Warmth of heart cannot make up for it."

Warmth of heart is often emphasized in essays on the Jesus Prayer, such as *Unseen Warfare,* or *The Way of the Pilgrim.* I think that Simone Weil is warning against prayer as a pleasurable, self-satisfying emotion, rather than total attentiveness to God and his will, no matter how startling that may sometimes be.

Sometimes the Jesus Prayer does surprise and turn me

around, but mostly it is a beautiful part of that rhythm which is with me not only when I am on retreat, but during that "damn dailiness" which is the largest part of our lives.

William Johnston writes in *The Mirror Mind* that "we must carefully distinguish between a word that is truly religious and one that is magical. In authentic religion the power of the word resides not in the sound itself but in the faith of the speaker. In magic, on the other hand, the power resides in the word itself—hence what counts is the use of the correct formula, correctly pronounced, and this formula must be kept a dark secret, since anyone who knows it automatically possesses the power. It is this magical use of words (as well as the mechanical repetition of sounds) that Jesus castigates when he says, 'And in praying do not heap up empty phrases as the Gentiles do; for they think that they will be heard for their many words.'. . . I emphasize this because magical formulas have been used in certain forms of oriental meditation that have been introduced to the West, and magic is to be avoided by anyone who would practise authentic religion."

Certainly I have never attempted to count the number of times the Jesus Prayer repeats itself within me during the day and night. There is no more virtue to be found in saying it a million times than half a million. I share Father Johnston's sensitivity about turning religion into magic (If I say the Jesus Prayer ten thousand times then God will give me thus and so); but I also believe that there is more power in the words of the Jesus Prayer than in my own fragile faith. When my spiritual director gave me this prayer I was still trying (and failing) to understand the incarnation with my intellect. Jesus is wholly God and wholly man?!? Jesus is exactly like us, except sinless?!? Jesus came to save us from our sins and from the Father?!?

My mind was running into intellectual brick walls. But

I had been trained in college to use my mind. Even though I had majored in English literature, I was trained to be suspicious of anything which was beyond the realm of logic. And so I was suspicious of the incarnation; I was suspicious of accepting Christ as Lord.

My spiritual director knew this when he gave me the Jesus Prayer. He offered it to me not as an easy solution to my problems, but gently, tentatively, as a gift. And because I trusted him I was willing at least to open the gift, look at it, try it on. And so, not really believing in Jesus, I started to live with the Jesus Prayer. And the power of the prayer itself moved from beyond the limitations of the intellect and into my heart.

I never stumbled into the error of thinking of the prayer as some kind of magic formula. I knew only that I was lost and that I needed to be found. My finding was not magic; it was miracle. And miracle comes from God. Human beings can use magic, sometimes for good, sometimes for evil; it has great power. But miracle is wholly God's, and miracle, the particular miracle of the Jesus Prayer, made me understand as never before that all power belongs to God.

With man it is impossible. With God nothing is impossible.

Magic: I find I'm not really sure what magic is. An old woman growing healing herbs in her backyard and brewing them into tea for ailing children is not practising magic; she is practising an old and valid form of medicine. People who do not know the virtue in healing herbs can wrongly confuse the posset with magic. Magic is simply using what God has created, using it to do the things God created it to do. The problem arises when people forget that the power is God's and give it to a human being, or to whatever the human being is using. Magic becomes bad when a human being takes the credit for it. The focus should be on God, the Giver of the gift, otherwise something which is intrinsically good will be turned into something which is at the least dangerous, and at worst downright evil.

The Old Testament prepares us for the gift of the Jesus Prayer. In Deuteronomy we read:

> *And these words which I command you this day shall be upon your heart; and you shall teach them diligently to your children, and shall talk of them when you sit in your house, and when you walk by the way, and when you lie down, and when you rise. And you shall bind them as a sign upon your hand, and they shall be as frontlets between your eyes. And you shall write them on the doorposts of your house and on your gates.*

God's Word shall be everywhere in your life, in all parts of your living, in your downsitting and your uprising. The continual trust in the Word of God is not limited to the Jew or the Christian. It is part of the longing of the human psyche in all cultures. The Kalahari bushmen listen for it in the tapping of the stars. The Buddhist believes that the "proper recitation of the sutra is a way of salvation not only for the one who recites but also for his relatives and friends", writes William Johnston in *The Mirror Mind*.

And in all cultures it is made clear that the recitation of the holy words is never for the individual; it is for the salvation of all people, the redemption of the entire universe. The interrelationship is so total that at the death of a single person the galaxies quake. And the laughter of one child is part of the singing of the stars.

———◆◆◆———

Nevertheless I would like all the answers re my prayer life, my spiritual life, handed me all tidily wrapped up. But I have learned that if I want neat, unconflicting answers, I would have to go to some rigid sect where my free will would be denied. And so I have learned to rejoice in questions.

I left the Episcopal Church, the church of my birth, after six years of Anglican boarding schools. In college I opted for the world of the intellect, where mind alone was going to conquer all. I read philosophy, taught by a brilliant atheist, and found that I still longed for God, and so did the philosophers.

My return to the church was not easy. It was a difficult journey of painful questions and painful happenings. I had to live through illness, and through the death of some close to me. I had to live through more than a decade of rejection for my work. And a near decade of living year round in a rural setting, while we had our family, ran a general store in the village, and I was forced to face all the questions to which I found no answers, and which I learned, agonizingly, *had* no answers. Not in mortal terms.

At a writers' conference a young woman stood up and said, "I read *A Wrinkle in Time* when I was about eight, and I didn't understand it. But I knew what it was about." And that remark, too, was a revelation to me.

At a church conference recently someone asked, "You have referred to your agnostic period. What happened to get you out of it?"

And I reply, joyfully, that I am still an agnostic, but then I was an unhappy one, seeking finite answers, and now I am a happy one, rejoicing in paradox. *Agnostic* means only that we do not *know*, and we finite creatures cannot know, in any intellectual or ultimate way, the infinite Lord, the undivided Trinity. Now I am able to accept my not-knowing—and yet, in a completely different way, in the old biblical way, I also know what I do not understand, and that is what my agnosticism means to me now. It does not mean that I do not believe; it is an acceptance that I am created, that I am asked to bear the light, knowing that this is the most wonderful of all vocations.

When I returned to the church of my birth it was not to discard the intellect, but now I know that to depend on intellect alone is not enough. Perhaps it is because I am a story teller that I need sign, symbol, sacrament, that which takes me beyond where my mind can go alone.

I discover that I am most certain of who I am when I am paying least attention to myself, that I most enjoy the legitimate pleasures of this world when they are not uppermost in my mind. My prayer life is very up and down. I go through long dry periods, and although I know that these are part of faith, when I am lost in the dark night of the soul I fear that it is never going to end. I do know that I need to do my daily finger exercises of prayer, reading Morning and Evening Prayer and meditating on psalter and Scripture even when the words seem empty and my thoughts stupid. Sometimes the Jesus Prayer is like a slack rope. But if I do not do my finger exercises regularly, when the time comes for the words to be filled, they will not be there.

I wish that the church demanded more of us. The human psyche thrives on creative demands, and if we aren't given real ones, we fall for illegitimate ones, like those imposed by some of the sects and which can sometimes lead to horrors such as ritual suicide in Guyana. In order to receive and fulfill legitimate demands, I am an associate of the Community of the Holy Spirit, and following that rule is, far from being restrictive, wonderfully freeing. It is shape and pattern when the days are over-busy, or when I look for definitive answers and find none.

I don't think there are any. There certainly weren't for Abraham and Sarah.

Love's Hardest Lesson

9

SARAH BORE A SON, and his name was Isaac, and he was, not surprisingly, the apple of his parents' eye.

But before we get into the story of Isaac, we come to Sodom and Gomorrah. Since I was born in, and live for a good part of the year in the modern Sodom, I have a certain feeling for the destruction of great cities.

It was immediately after the laughter of Sarah, and while the three heavenly visitors were getting ready to leave Abraham and Sarah, that

> *the Lord said, Because the noise of Sodom and Gomorrah is very great, and because their sin is very grievous, I will go down now*

and see if they are truly as wicked as they seem to be.

So the three heavenly visitors turned away from Abraham and Sarah on the plain of Mamre, and looked towards Sodom.

> *But Abraham stood in front of the Lord and said, Will you also destroy the righteous along with the wicked? Possibly there are fifty righteous people within the city. Will you go ahead and destroy? Or will you spare the place for the sake of the fifty righteous ... Shall not the judge of all the earth do right?*

Powerful language for Abraham to use before the Lord of the universe, but the prophets, for all their faults and flaws, had the courage of their convictions, and Abraham's conviction was that the Lord had to do what is right, that what el did must *be* right. Perhaps this encounter with divine judgment over Sodom and Gomorrah stood him in good stead later on.

> *And the Lord said, If I find in Sodom fifty innocent people, I will spare the whole city for their sake.*

Abraham continued to push. "Forgive me—but what if there are only forty-five innocent people?" and then forty, and then thirty, and then twenty, and then ten—and each time the Lord said that el would save the city for the sake of the innocent people.

A wonderful conversation, a freeing conversation. There is nothing we need be afraid to say before the Lord.

———◆◆———

So I continued to read, to think, to pray. And by the time our freighter holiday was over, I was so deep in Genesis that wherever I went I reached for whatever Bible, in whatever translation was available, and continued to read, to think, and to hope that what I read and thought would move me on into prayer.

———◆◆———

After this remarkable conversation about the wicked inhabitants of Sodom and Gomorrah, God went along, and Abraham, having had his say about the innocent people, went home, and Jehovah left the two angels to complete the mission he'd given them. They left Mamre and went to Sodom, where Lot, Abraham's nephew, was sitting at the city gate. He greeted the two angels, who were in the form of two beautiful young men, and after some persuasion on Lot's part they went to his house where he had a fine meal prepared for them, which they ate. Angels may be pure energy, but these angels made a point of eating so that people would understand that they were real (energy and matter are, we now understand, interchangeable; nevertheless this proof of reality for our sakes is amazing). And as the resurrected Christ made a point of eating fish and bread and drinking wine, so that his friends would know that he was real, even if they failed to recognize him by sight.

So the angels ate the meal Lot offered them. At bedtime all the men in the city, young and old, surrounded Lot's house and asked him to bring the two young men to them. According to the King James translation, the men of Sodom wanted to "know" the two young men, in the same sense that Adam "knew" Eve. The *Good News Bible*, which was the translation in my room when I came to this part of the story, puts it very bluntly. They wanted

to have sex with them.

Lot, of course, was horrified. It was his ingrained habit of hospitality which had caused him to ask the two young men home for a meal, nothing else.

He went outside and closed the door behind him. He said to them, "Friends, I beg you, don't do such a wicked thing!"

The sacredness of hospitality, and of one's responsibility towards one's guests was far greater then than it is now. It is difficult for us to understand Lot's feeling of obligation towards these two strangers whom he felt he must protect at all costs. Of course, he didn't know that they were angels and well able to protect themselves; therefore he could not betray his sacred obligation. Even so, his response seems extreme. Lot offered the men of Sodom his two daughters, which may have been wily, rather than naive, under the circumstances, adding,

> *"But don't do anything with these men; they are guests in my house and I must protect them." But the men of Sodom said, "Get out of the way, you foreigner!"*

Distrust of foreigners seems to be as old as the fear of great darkness, and probably came about because foreigners, if they were stronger than you, were apt to take your land and your wives and make you into slaves. However, Lot surely posed no threat to Sodom.

When the men of that city would have forced their way into Lot's house by breaking down the door, the two angels

> *pulled Lot back into the house and shut the door. Then they struck all the men outside with blindness.*
>
> *The two men said to Lot, "If you have anyone else here, sons, daughters, sons-in-law or any other relatives living in the city, get them out of here, because we are going to destroy this place." . . .*

So Lot went to the men his daughters were engaged to and said, "Hurry up and get out of here! The Lord is going to destroy this place."

For by now he understood that the two men were angels.

Where were the ten just men for whom Abraham had begged the Lord to save the city? It seems that there were not even ten just men in that great city.

According to Hassidic tradition, there are always ten just men in the world (and once again I am using the word *men* in the generic, biblical sense of male and female). These ten just people do not know who they are. Only God knows. When one dies, the place is filled by another. So long as there are ten just men...

But there were not ten just men in Sodom, and in the morning the angels took Lot,

his wife, and his two daughters, by the hand and led them out of the city. Then one of the angels said, "Run for your lives! Don't look back and don't stop in the valley. Run to the hills so that you won't be killed!"

God's people are ever argumentative. Lot thanked the angels for saving their lives, but argued that the hills were too far away.

"Do you see that little town? It is near enough. Let me go over there. You can see that it is just a small place. And I will be safe."

The angel answered, "All right, I agree. I won't destroy that town. Hurry! Run!"

And at last Lot ran. The sun was already beginning to rise when Lot reached the little town which was named

Zoar. Suddenly the Lord rained burning sulphur on the cities of Sodom and Gomorrah and destroyed them and the whole valley along with all the people there and everything that grew on the land. But Lot's wife looked back and was turned into a pillar of salt.

Sodom had been their home. It was a natural enough thing for her to want to take one last look. And if Lot hadn't argued with the angel, and so delayed their departure, she might have been all right.

In Pompeii one can see the petrified forms of people who had been caught in the grey ash of the volcano, perhaps also looking back for one last glimpse of home, and who were turned, not into salt, but into statues of volcanic rock.

Early the next morning Abraham hurried to the place where he had stood in the presence of the Lord. He looked down on Sodom and Gomorrah and the whole valley and saw smoke rising from the land, like smoke from a huge furnace.

The destruction of Sodom and Gomorrah, whatever caused it, sounds terrifyingly like the destruction which would be caused by atomic warfare.

At a dinner party I sat next to someone who works for the Army Corps of Engineers, and whose present job is planning the evacuation of New York city, and the feeding and housing of survivors, *after* the city has been hit by an atomic bomb. This person is receiving a government pay check for this effort in futility, and I could not help exploding, "The thing to do is to *stop* an atom bomb from falling on New York in the first place, not figure out how to feed and house people after they're dead, or dying of radiation sickness."

I still believe that atomic warfare can be prevented, as long as there are ten just men left in the world. As I continue to type out for my children some of the loveliness of their childhoods, trying to cull from my journals the delicate flowers from the overgrowth of rank weeds, and reliving the years of raising a family and struggling to write, I also live through the continuing series of past international crises. One spring back in the fifties when the serious news commentators did not think it likely that we would make it through the summer without hostilities breaking out between the Soviet Union and the United States, I walked down our dirt road picking pussy willows and wondering if this was the last time I would see the loveliness of spring trembling across the land. In school the children were taught how to hide under their desks, with their hands over their heads, and I was shocked at the folly of it, for how could the wood of a desk protect these little ones from even an ordinary bomb?

So I shudder when people link atomic destruction with the Parousia, the Second Coming. It seems to me that it trivializes Christ's Second Coming to assume that it involves this planet only, or could be caused by the folly of power-greedy man. If we take seriously that Christ was the Word who spoke creation into being, if we take seriously that

In the beginning was the Word, and the Word was with God, and the Word was God . . . All things were made by him, and without him was not anything made that was made—

all things, all of the galaxies with their countless trillions of solar systems—if we truly believe this, then the Second Coming is not for this planet alone. It is for all of creation.

When we concentrate on ourselves, on planet earth, we

stumble into the old Greek flaw—a fatal one—of hubris. We play into the hands of Satan, and also of the various extreme sects which assume that they, and they alone, of all of God's creation, are to be saved. It is a presumptuous thing, and very seductive one, to decide that you and your group are the sheep destined for heaven, and all the rest, including Anglicans like me, are destined for hell fire.

My children and grandchildren have never known a world which was not under the shadow of the mushroom cloud. It is hard for them to realize that when I was a child there was no Pentagon. It is hard for me to realize that, too, as I look through those old journals, and decide that when I finish culling things for children and grandchildren they had better be burned.

If we continue our arrogant ways until we incinerate this planet, it will be we foolish creatures who are doing it, not God. We need to rid ourselves of the megalomania which focuses God's prime concern on this one minuscule part of creation. Not that we aren't important; we are. *All* of creation is important. If we blow ourselves up it will likely have negative effects on planets in distant galaxies.

Are we grown up enough to use the power we have discovered in the atom creatively instead of destructively? Are we capable of holding back on this use until we have learned how to dispose of atomic waste? And what about those containers of atomic waste which are already lying on the bottom of the ocean and which are beginning to rust, so that radiation is seeping out and spreading its contamination?

We have discovered this incredible power at the heart of the atom, and we can't make it go away. And we, like Adam and Eve, are still out of synchronization. We know, with our intellects, much more than we can comprehend with our spirits. We are woefully, terrifyingly, out of balance.

I do believe in the Second Coming, the fulfillment of all

things, but not that it is tied in with man's ability to turn the earth into a dead, dark satellite. I do not think that God collaborates with us creatures in destruction. That's Satan's realm. God calls us to be co-creators with el. If we refuse this high calling, then we—in one way or another—destroy ourselves. Like the people of Sodom.

And what about those people of Sodom? Do I want even the most depraved sodomite to be destroyed forever?

There are crimes so vile that they are totally beyond my ability either to assess or to forgive. In ancient Hebrew times when someone was put outside the city walls it was because he had done something so terrible that the tribe could not punish it, and so the sinner was handed over to God. "This is beyond us, Lord. We're delivering him to you."

There is a club in New York, membership in which depends on the ability to find and produce a white man's testicles, and little boys are the easiest victims. I know about this only because it happened to someone we knew of. After my first murderous reaction, I realized that it is beyond anything I can understand or respond to. And the very perpetrators of this crime have had, or their ancestors have had, equally vile horrors done them by white men. Evil spawns evil.

A plague on both your houses! Mercutio cried. Outside the city walls! Only God can deal with this.

What can we human beings do with an Eichmann? Or the doctors in the concentration camps who made lamp-shades out of human skin, who turned children into soap? There is *nothing* we could do which would be adequate punishment.

But what is punishment?

There is only one purpose for punishment, and that is to teach a lesson, and there is only one lesson to be taught, and that is love. Perfect love banishes fear and when we are not afraid we know that love which includes forgiveness. When the lesson to be learned is not love, that is not punishment; it is revenge, or retribution. Probably the lesson of love is the most terrible punishment of all—an almost intolerable anguish—for it means that the sinner has to realize what has been done, has to be truly sorry, to repent, to turn to God. And most of us are too filled with outrage at rape and murder to want the sinner to repent. We want the sinner to feel terrible, but not to turn to God, and be made whole and be forgiven. And so we show that we do not know the meaning of forgiveness, any more than Jonah did in his vindictive outrage at the people of Nineveh.

We are so familiar with the Parable of the Prodigal Son that we forget part of the message, and that is the response of the elder brother. As I read and reread Scripture it seems evident that God is far more loving than we are, and far more forgiving. We do not want God to forgive our enemies, but Scripture teaches us that all God wants is for us to repent, to say, "I'm sorry, Father. Forgive me," as the Prodigal Son does when he *comes to himself* and recognizes the extent of his folly and wrongdoing. And the father rejoices in his return.

Then there's the elder brother. We don't like to recognize ourselves in the elder brother who goes off and sulks because the father, so delighted at the return of the younger brother, prepares a great feast. Punishment? A party! Because the younger brother has learned the lesson he has, in a sense, already punished himself. But, like the elder brother, we're apt to think the father much too lenient.

When our children were little they used to do what I called "working up to a spanking." It usually took about two weeks, and quite a few warnings. One time our eldest child had worked herself up to a spanking and been given one, and that night she sat in her father's lap, twined her arms about his neck, and said, "Daddy, why is it I'm so much nicer after I've been spanked?"

Because it was a lesson of love, that's why. I did not spank my children when I was angry; when I was angry I was incapable of teaching that lesson of love. If I was really angry, I would say, "Go sit in your room until I have calmed down enough to talk with you. I don't want to talk while I'm angry."

And our younger daughter once asked me, "Mother, are you mad *at* me, or mad *with* me?"

"I'm mad with you," I replied. She was right; there is a big difference.

So whatever punishment God gives us when we do wrong, it is to teach us a lesson of love. And, just as we do not enjoy punishing our children, God does not enjoy punishing us. But that hard lesson of love must be learned.

The Book of Common Prayer includes Manasseh's Song of Repentance:

> *O Lord and Ruler of the hosts of heaven,*
> *God of Abraham, Isaac, and Jacob,*
> *and of all their righteous offspring:*
> *You made the heavens and the earth*
> *with all their vast array.*
> *All things quake with fear at your presence;*
> *they tremble because of your power.*
> *But your merciful promise is beyond all measure;*
> *it surpasses all that our minds can fathom.*
> *O Lord, you are full of compassion,*
> *long-suffering, and abounding in mercy.*
> *You hold back your hand;*
> *you do not punish as we deserve.*
> *In your great goodness, Lord,*

you have promised forgiveness to sinners,
    that they may repent of their sin and be saved.
And now, O Lord, I bend the knee of my heart,
    and make my appeal, sure of your gracious goodness.
I have sinned, O Lord, I have sinned,
    and I know my wickedness only too well.
Therefore I make this prayer to you:
    Forgive me, Lord, forgive me.
Do not let me perish in my sin,
    nor condemn me to the depths of the earth.
For you, O Lord, are the God of those who repent,
    and in me you will show forth your goodness.
Unworthy as I am, you will save me,
in accordance with your great mercy,
    and I will praise you without ceasing all the
    days of my life.
For all the powers of heaven sing your praises,
    and yours is the glory to ages of ages. Amen.

How wonderful to know that God forgives us when we come to ourselves and understand whatever it is that we have done and ask for forgiveness. Perhaps it is the quality of repentance which counts, not the magnitude of the sin. I must bend the knee of my heart and beg God's forgiveness as fervently as did the Prodigal Son, though my sins may be far less flamboyant. Perhaps the Sodomites had gone, in this life, beyond repentance. In any case, Lot probably felt that they got no more than their due.

But that's the elder brother syndrome. And it's a disease, a contagious disease.

So there's no avoiding my bumping headlong into the accusation of universalism.

And I am not, repeat, am *not* a universalist.

I used to think, when people worried about whether or

not I am a universalist, that a universalist was someone who believes that Jesus is good, and Buddha is good, and Mohammed is good, and that all ways to Heaven are equal, and I wondered where on earth they had got this odd idea about me.

It took me nearly five years to figure this out. As far as I can gather, universalism means that all of a sudden, and for no particular reason, God is going to wave a magic wand, and say, "Okay, everybody, out of hell. Home free."

Now that I know what it means, I can, and do, reply, "No, I am certainly not a universalist. That plays trivially with free will." And about God's great and terrible gift of free will I feel very strongly indeed.

At one southern university one young man, who had asked the inevitable question, pushed me further. "But you do seem to indicate, in your writing, that you believe in God's forgiveness?"

That seemed to me an extraordinary question, considering that it came from a student in a Christian college.

Fortunately, he qualified it. "You seem to believe that ultimately God is going to forgive *everybody?*"

I said, "I don't believe that God is going to fail with el's creation. I don't worship a failing God. Do you want God to fail?"

He said, "But there has to be *absolute* justice."

"You're maybe nineteen or twenty years old. When you die, is that what you want—absolute justice? Don't you want the teeniest, weeniest bit of mercy? Me, I want lots and lots of mercy. Don't you feel that you're going to need any mercy at all?"

That had not occurred to him. So he started to quote Scripture. I stopped him. "I can quote Scripture, too. Let's start with Ezekiel. In the thirty-third chapter, the tenth verse, Ezekiel says:

*"Son of man, say to the House of Israel, 'You are con-
tinually saying: Our sins and crimes weigh heavily on us;
we are wasting away because of them. How are we to go
on living?' Say to them, 'As I live—it is the Lord who
speaks—I take pleasure, not in the death of a wicked
man, but in the turning back of a wicked man who
changes his ways to win life. Come back, come back
from your evil ways. Why are you so anxious to die,
House of Israel?'*

*"And you, son of man, say to the members of your
nation, 'The integrity of an upright man will not save
him once he has chosen to sin; the wickedness of a
wicked man will no longer condemn him once he renounces wickedness... All his precious sins will no
longer be remembered...*

*"The members of your nation object: 'What the Lord
does is unjust;' but it is what you do that is unjust. When
an upright man renounces his integrity and commits
sin, he dies for it. And when a wicked man renounces
his wickedness and does what is lawful and right, because of this he lives."*

These must have been comfortable words to Paul, who surely would not have done well when judged by men's stan-
dards of absolute justice. He had cheered on the stoning of
Stephen; he had caused many Christians to be put to death.
He had a great deal of blood on his hands. But he repented.
He turned around completely, and served the Lord he had
been denying and denouncing.

So I suggested to the young man that he go to Scripture,
to Genesis 1, and read straight through to the end of John's
revelation, and set down on a pad all that speaks of God's
mercy and loving forgiveness versus all that shows el's anger
and wrath, and see which came out most clearly. The sulki-

ness of the elder brother is pointed out to us again and again as being the opposite of God's loving forgiveness.

I don't know when or how it is going to happen, but don't give up on me: God is not finished with me yet. Nor with you. Nor—whether we like it or not, for we have hard hearts—the Sodomites. Nor any part of creation. For we are God's, a part of creation, a part of that which God made and called good. The story of Adam and Eve, and all the stories which follow, show us what we have done to that good, fouled and desecrated it; but that which God created is good, and, as John points out:

> *Anyone who fails to love can never have known God, because God is love. God's love for us was revealed when God sent into the world his only Son so that we could have life through him; this is the love I mean: not our love for God, but God's love for us when he sent his Son to be the sacrifice that takes our sins away.*

God's love is not easy for us elder brothers to accept. A party for the sinner! Horrors!

When I do something which is less than God expects of me, I am miserable. Accepting that I have done wrong is excruciatingly painful. Often it is even more difficult for me to forgive myself than it is to accept God's forgiveness for me. My own acknowledgment of my wrongdoing is the most difficult punishment possible. Repentance is neither easy nor cheap. It hurts. It costs us all our pride and self-will. It means letting go completely and handing ourselves back to God. To hand God our sins is far more difficult than any other kind of prayer, and yet it is one of the most important parts of prayer. And when I can completely let it go, let God take it, and redeem it, and transform it, then I, too, am ready for a party!

It is difficult to express a seriously thought-out point of view in an area where there are no final answers, without appearing to make a final answer, a definitive and lasting judgment. No one of us can read the mind of God. I know only that through a lifetime of reading and rereading Scripture I have come to believe that "mercy and truth have kissed each other" and that God's love is beyond our puny comprehension.

Job asked God the finite questions we all ask, and God replied,

> *Where were you when I laid the foundations of the earth? Tell me, if you understand it. Who measured it out, and stretched the line upon it? Where are the foundations of the earth? Who laid the cornerstone when the morning stars sang together and all God's children shouted for joy?*

That was not the answer Job was looking for, but it was the answer God gave.

If eternal damnation is part of our mindset, it is far too easy to wonder if part of the joy of the saved in heaven is looking down on the tortures of the damned. How unlike the shepherd who left the ninety-nine saved sheep and went in search of the single one who was lost!

Most of the passages in the New Testament which imply eternal damnation (Dives and Lazarus; the wheat and the tares) are in parables, and parables are stories. Jesus often used hyperbole when he wanted to make a point. Are we to believe that someone actually had a plank of wood in his eyes, or that Jesus really recommended the dishonest wheeling and dealing of the unjust steward? Did he really expect a father to consider giving a scorpion instead of an egg to his child? "But if you, who are only a human father, are good to your children, how much more loving is the heavenly Father!"

Jesus did not speak in the language of proof, but in the language of story. We can neither prove nor disprove the existence of God. But if we examine human perception of God as it is revealed, bit by bit, through Scripture, the un-qualified love of the Creator for creation and for all of us creatures is paramount. Is it unfair for me to equate the mind that looks for porn with the mind that looks for damnation? I'd much rather look for wonder and salvation! Is Gandhi to be excluded from heaven because he never made a formal commitment to Christ? Gandhi, who was thrown out of a Christian church because his skin was not the "right" colour? We have much to answer for, we Christians, and excluding part of God's family from God's church is a big problem How do we solve it?

Jesus walked and talked with those who, like Gandhi, were considered not quite good enough for the establishment of his day: the Samaritans, the wretchedly poor and ill, fallen women, lepers. It was of such "disqualified" people that Jesus said, "I have come not to heal those who are well, but those who are ill."

I am a flawed human being in need of this healing. I dread to think what I would be like if I felt much more saved than other people (often people far better than I, but who have not accepted Christ), that I could think I had a greater right to heaven than they. And those who are worse. I have never raped, murdered, committed adultery, the more spectacular sins. I think of God's words to Job, to Jonah. I think of the Good Shepherd who cannot rest until he has found the one lost sheep. I think of the Prodigal Son who ultimately repented of his folly, of his own free will. Perhaps he repented only because he was starving and thought of all the food his father's servants had to eat, but repent he did, and his father threw a party, and his elder brother stamped his foot and sulked because this repentant sinner was admitted to heaven.

Knowing that we cannot define God, why do we try to put limits on el? How can we limit el's love? It is we who are limited, not God. I cannot believe that God's unlimited love (and that limitlessness is shown in the incarnation), will not outlast all our rebellion and anger and independence and brutality and indifference and hubris and all that keeps us from turning to him.

I suggest Jonah as bedtime reading every night for a month or so. Jonah doesn't want God to save the enemy, the Ninevites, who aren't on "our side," even if they repent of their sins. And God reminds Jonah that Jonah spared a worm, so why should el not spare the Ninevites who do not know their left hand from their right, and also much cattle?

------◆◆◆------

After the destruction of Sodom nobody is ready for a party. The scene is grim indeed. And then follows a passage so shocking it is often deleted, for public reading. Lot and his daughters

> moved up into the hills and lived in a cave. The elder daughter said to her sister, "Our father is getting old, and there are no men in the whole world to marry us so that we can have children. Come on, let's make our father drunk, so that we can sleep with him and have children by him."

That's the *Good News Bible.* The *King James Version* has it:

> Come, let us make our father drink wine, and we will lie with him, that we may preserve the seed of our father.

"Preserving the seed" is closer to the intent of the thinking of the time. At moments of devastation the old taboos break down. The instinct for survival, for the propagation of the species, is stronger than the taboo. In our generation we remember the plane which crashed in the snow, high up in the Andes; the starving survivors ultimately had to eat the bodies of their dead companions to avoid starvation. Again, under such extreme circumstances the taboo no longer held.

So

That night Lot's daughters gave him wine to drink, and the older daughter had intercourse with him. But he was so drunk that he didn't know it.

I was in Covington, Louisiana, while I was reading about Lot and meditating upon his story, so I'll stay with the Bible in my room there, the *Good News Bible,* for a while.

The next day the elder daughter said to her sister, "I slept with him last night. Now let's make him drunk again tonight, and you sleep with him. Then each of us will have a child by our father."

Pragmatic, practical young women, like their great-uncle Abraham. They both had sons, who became the ancestors of the Moabites and the Ammonites, and we remember the Moabites because of the story of Ruth, who was from Moab, and through whom Jesus' genealogy is traced.

But where are the Moabites now? War. Holocaust. Genocide. What has happened to the Moabites and the Ammonites, the Hittites and the Amalakites? Gone, gone without a trace; a sad reminder that throughout earth's history civilizations rise and fall. Ozymandias is an example of the consequence of human pride.

———◆◆◆———

One of the most fascinating aspects of reading the Old Testament is to see the perception of God changing throughout the ages, so that the Abba to whom Jesus prayed is seen as different from the tribal god who helped Israel's kings destroy entire nations and peoples in order to give the land to the Israelites. (Are *most* wars over land boundaries?)

God's anger with David for not killing *everybody* has always bothered me, and the explanation that it was necessary to keep the children of Israel from worshiping the gods of the enemy has never seemed quite satisfactory. Then I remember that people were then, as now, struggling with finite minds to comprehend an infinite God. Anything we can say about God is going to be inadequate, a groping for truths beyond our limited capacities.

And (paradox again) I believe in the Bible as the living Word of God. But this faith involves an acceptance that the Bible is not static; that at different times the living Word can speak in different ways to different ears, and that even the Bible itself can never fully express or manifest the glory of the Creator. That does not make it any less the living Word. It is because it lives that it moves.

Listen: this is the song of the great prophet, Moses:

The Lord is a mighty warrior;
The chariots of Pharoah and his army has he hurled into
the sea;
the finest of those who bear armour have been drowned
in the Red Sea.
The fathomless deep has overwhelmed them; they sank
into the depths like a stone.
Your right hand, O Lord, is glorious in might; your
right hand, O Lord, has overthrown the enemy.

> *You stretched forth your right hand; the earth swallowed them up.*

"Is that vengeful God the Lord whom Jesus called Abba, and was faithful to?" I was asked.

Well, the song of triumph over the death of enemies, the praise to the Lord for killing our oppressors, upset even the oppressed, the children of Israel who were so ill-treated by Pharoah and the Egyptians.

And, as usual, when something is beyond us, we try to look for understanding in story. This one comes, I think, out of the Hassidic tradition, but it says everything that needs to be said about the Song of Moses:

The Israelites flee Egypt, and the waters of the Red Sea open, and they go through on dry land, and are safe on the other side. The Egyptians in their chariots pursue them, and dash into the open path where the waters have rolled back, and as soon as they are all in the sea, the waters close over them, and they all drown.

And in heaven, joyful at the narrow escape of the Jewish people, the angels start to sing. And God stops them, saying:

"How can you sing when my children are dying?"

We must try to keep our receivers tuned finely so that we will not drown out revelation with static, and thus set our perception of God in concrete, unable to change.

The revelation given me when the words, "My religion is subject to change without notice," came unbidden from my lips, was not trivial. For this openness is what we should practice, with religion as well as science. Abraham and Sarah lived with this child-like ability to change, to leave the known, to go out into the wilderness, and God didn't give them much notice.

The discoveries of the quantum physicists have done nothing to change the nature of the universe, but they have changed, radically, our way of perceiving the universe. There is nothing static. We change each other simply by observing each other. We are all part of something far greater than we can begin to comprehend, and to be part of the changing melody and the complexity of the dance is part of our vocation as co-creators.

In both Old and New Testaments, the institution of slavery is taken for granted. Now we could consider it intolerable in God's eyes, so far has our perception of God changed. We have moved from seeing God as one who favours one part of creation over the rest of it, to a God who is Lord of all.

In this century we are moving from an impassible God who cannot suffer to an Abba who shares all our pain with us, who hurts when we hurt, who not only notes but *feels* the fall of every sparrow. And who steadily and gently guides us to a wider understanding of love.

As our love for our Maker grows, so does our love for each other. In our society we can no longer tolerate having indentured servants. The idea of the "white man's burden" seems arrogant and self-serving, though there are still many who treat people of other races not only as inferiors, but as less important in God's eyes than they themselves are. We know that greed makes the skies and the seas more polluted than they need be, though we know how to clean up our wastes, since we have brought a dead Great Lake and the great Hudson River back to life. Why do things have to reach a desperate state before we do anything about them? In many ways we are as inturned and shortsighted as the captains and crews of the great whaling ships, though we see the wrong they did better than we see our own wrongdoing. We can guess that later generations will see our sins more clearly than they see their own. We all get trapped in chronology.

But in God's time, in kairos, all is *now,* is present. Part of the joy of silence, of meditation and contemplation, is to touch on this *is*-ness. In God's mind, nothing is lost. All acts of love are eternally present. And all that is not love can be redeemed and changed by that Love which created all.

Sometimes we human beings are allowed to touch on kairos.

While I was in Covington, reading the story of Lot, then moving on to Abraham and Sarah and Isaac, I was given one of these revelations of divine love. It came in a dream, the kind I call a Special Dream.

There are, by and large, three kinds of dreams. There is the dream which is easy to translate, which comes from something we have eaten, or some recent event. Then there is the regular dream, which is more difficult to understand. Dreams do have messages for us, which we do well to take seriously, but I don't want to get faddish about them. If I wake from a dream in the night and think it may have something to say to me, I ask my subconscious mind to surface it for me in the morning, and it usually does.

The Special Dream is different. It, like prayer, is a gift.

The retreat center at Covington is part of a much larger complex. There is a seminary, a school, a church. As I was being driven through the grounds to the retreat center I could see that a service was about to begin at the church, for a large group of people of all ages was going up the steps and through the doors. And I was told that it was a funeral for a high school senior who had died in an inexplicable automobile accident; her car had been found slammed into a tree. As so often seems to be the case when someone dies young, she had been a popular and happy girl, with an excellent academic record, expected to be able to get into any college to which she applied. No one knew what had happened to make her car go out of control. And she was an only child.

A chill shadow was cast over the day.

Then I was being shown through the beautiful retreat center; the retreatants began to arrive; I joyfully met old friends, was introduced to new. Because I was fully in each present moment of the retreat, everything else faded.

At the end of the evening I went gratefully to bed, read for a few minutes, and went to sleep. Perhaps I had been thinking about God taking Abraham out at night and showing him the stars. I slept, and I dreamed. A Special Dream. Many such dreams are golden. This one was diamond.

It was a gorgeous night, and I was outside with many of the people who were on the retreat. I was joyfully looking at the stars which were clustered far more densely than usual, in brilliant, intricate patterns. Suddenly, in the east, there was a child of light, of dazzling light, and all the stars began to dance about the child in joy. And we were part of that joy.

That was the dream. I didn't remember it on first waking, but something brought it flashing up to my conscious mind. And I realized that I had been given the gift of a resurrection dream.

And I knew that the girl who had died was part of that glory and part of that joy. For the brief moments of a sleeping dream I had been caught up in that love which is eternal and knows no restrictions of time.

God is omnipotent. All time is in el's hand. Past, present, future.

So what (the question asks itself once again) does that do to our free will?

And again the astrophysicist, rather than the theologian

(though I am well aware that there are many poor astrophysicists, just as there are many poor theologians) comes to my rescue. As God created time to be free, so el created us to be free. As we are capable of change, so is time. What we do is going to make a difference to the future, may change the future. And here we come to an astrophysical theory which is so extraordinary it is hardly conceivable: what we do may change not only the future; it is possible that it may change the past.

How? Well, there are many theories, such as alternate universes and time warps. But that time is free, past time as well as future, is being put forth as a serious theory, and it is the theory behind *A Swiftly Tilting Planet.*

Possibly I am reading more theology into astrophysics than the scientists intend, but if there is no dichotomy between sacred and secular, then everything is theological, from a solitary hot soak in the tub to the dance of the galaxies to the changing of a diaper. The new theories of time certainly leave us with more questions than answers; but allowing ourselves to move from question to question, knowing that in this life we are not likely to find all the definitive answers, is part of prayer.

Impossibilities That Happen
10

IN OUR DAILY READING of Scripture, when we move from reading to thinking and, if the gift is given, from thinking to praying, it is not surprising, nor is it bad that we often find ourselves far from the original verses which have triggered our thoughts.

Surely Sarah prayed for a child. Perhaps she argued with God, cried out to el in anguish and anger. Why was Hagar able to conceive when Sarah was not? Why was Hagar's response smugness and pride with herself, and scorn towards Sarah?

Perhaps Sarah even tried to bargain with God. Is that not one of the first things the tempter taught us? And one of the saddest?

But what were her prayers all about? Did God even hear them? And, if el heard, why did el not heed them? Why was the answer always *no?*

And then, of course, came the miracle.

And I think of some of the miracles of my own life.

Many happenings in my life are beyond reasonable understanding. But that they happened there is no doubt. One of the most amazing and the most glorious has to do with prayer, my prayer, bad prayer. At least, it was the kind of prayer I had been taught to believe was bad. If I learned nothing else in those Anglican boarding schools, I did learn that we are never, ever, to say, "This isn't fair. This shouldn't have happened to me." Especially, most especially, we are not to say this to God. Not ever. No matter what.

When my children complained, "It's not fair," I told them that nobody had promised them life was going to be fair. And I thought that I, myself, had learned this lesson.

One spring I had some complicated eye surgery, done by my marvellous ophthalmologist. I also had some nasty foot surgery. Each of these operations would have meant three months out of my life, and as I could not see taking six months off, I talked the doctors into doing the foot surgery first, and ten days later, the eye surgery. Preferably a short time of intense unpleasantness than dragging it out, I thought.

I went home from the hospital with everything going well, pins sticking out of the toes of my right foot, and a patch on my right eye which I was to take off when I bathed.

After I'd been home about two weeks, we went to the ballet to see our ballet-dancing son, a young man who had become part of our family a few years earlier. We went out to dinner first; the ballet was beautiful, and it was a happy evening. We went home and started getting ready for bed. Because of the pins still sticking out of my toes, I had to get into the bathtub bottom first, the right leg hanging out of the side of the tub. (Fortunately we have a right-legged tub.)

While I was bathing, the phone rang. Hugh was in the shower down the hall, and I knew that he couldn't hear it. But when the phone rings at eleven-thirty at night, we answer it. There have been enough accidents and unexpected crises in our family so that I never just let a phone go on ringing. With some effort I heaved myself out of the tub and limped toward the phone. It stopped, after only three rings, so I knew it was not one of our children. They would have let it go on ringing.

I turned back to the bathroom. Perhaps because I was wet and slippery, I slipped and fell, hitting my eye, right on the wound, on the corner of a chest.

I kept saying, childishly, "Don't let anything have happened. Don't let me have hurt my eye. Don't let anything be wrong."

But the world which, day by day, had been slowly coming back into view, had disappeared into a yellow fog.

Hugh came out of the shower and I told him what had happened. (All this in the space of a shower!) He called my doctor, who told us to get to the emergency room at St. Luke's, fast. We dressed hurriedly, and took a taxi to the hospital. The emergency room of a city hospital is a lot like hell. Out of a loud speaker rock music was blaring. This may have been comforting to some people; it made me ready to scream my way up the walls.

And Hugh was surrounded, by both patients and nurses. Everybody wanted Dr. Tyler's autograph. At any other time I would have thought it was funny, but being very aware of the grave damage to my eye, and being very, very frightened, I wanted to get to the ophthalmological department *as soon as possible.*

Nothing happens quickly in an emergency room unless you are spouting blood. Having "Dr. Tyler" with me did help, because he was able to cut through some of the red tape as though he were a "real" doctor, not simply one out of a soap opera.

By the time that my eye was examined, the pressure in the eyeball had dropped to zero, meaning that the eye could collapse at any moment. This was further complicated by the fact that the eye was hemorrhaging internally. The doctor was honest with me; I was admitted to the hospital and prepped for an operation in the morning which I knew well might mean the removal of the eye.

It was the early hours of the morning by the time I was left alone. I had been given a sleeping pill which was supposed to knock out an elephant. It might as well have been a bread crumb, I was so wide awake, and so very aware of the seriousness of the situation, and my adrenalin was pumping full force. I tried to lie quietly, to pray quietly. I was grateful to the night nurse for her gentle concern. I tried to offer everything to God, not to be frightened.

And suddenly I heard myself saying in a loud voice, "Lord, have I ever, in all these years, have I ever once said: This isn't fair? Have I ever once said: This shouldn't have happened to me? You know I haven't. Well, now I'm saying it!"

After that outburst I was able to lie quietly, to rest on the strong lifeline of the Jesus Prayer for the rest of the seemingly endless night.

In the morning when the doctor came, the pressure in the eyeball was up to normal. Half of the hemorrhage had already absorbed. And this simply is not possible. But it happened.

My doctor said with amazement, "You're all right, and I'm going to send you home, but just in case, I want you to lie flat on your back for ten days."

At that time I was working on the final revisions of *Walking on Water*, and Hugh called Harold and Luci Shaw to tell them what had happened, and to warn them that there would be a ten-day delay. Immediately, Luci called me back.

"Madeleine," she said, "I feel strongly that this was demonic interference."

The idea of demonic interference has not been part of the Episcopal tradition for a long time, though once again the possibility of it is being recognized. And I remembered that when I had been teaching at a writers' conference in Nashville, Tennessee, a lovely young woman I had never seen before came up to me and said earnestly, "Madeleine, I want you to know that I pray for you every day. Your work has made you vulnerable to attack and you need protection."

I lay there, flat on my back, and it seemed to me likely that the protection had somehow slipped, but then the angels came in and drove out the demon and undid his mischief. It is as reasonable an explanation as any.

When I went to the doctor to be checked, the eyeball pressure was still normal, and the hemorrhage had completely absorbed. That quickly? Not possible. But it happened.

Now every morning I put in my contact lenses and the world comes into view and I cry out, "Miracle!" and "Thank You!" There has yet to come a morning when I've taken restored sight for granted, and I doubt if there ever will, for the difference between seeing a vague, general blur, and *seeing* is not only quantitative but qualitative. Daily it is miracle, and awe, and joy.

I am grateful to the young woman in Nashville for her prayers of protection, and for the prayers of many others, for it is my firm conviction that it is these loving prayers which have kept me seeing, and which go on keeping me seeing. And the miracle of prayer is daily as fresh as the first daffodil in spring.

177

As to the phone call which was the superficial cause of all this: it was to tell me that *A Swiftly Tilting Planet* had won one of the National Book Awards.

A sensitive question was asked me. "In regard to intercessory prayer, if one prays for healing for someone, and the healing occurs, can we conclude that the healing would not have occurred had the prayer not been offered?"

Again, there is no easy answer, for if the healing would have occurred anyhow, why pray?

So we approach the mystery of intercessory prayer. George MacDonald answers one question with another: "And why should the good of anyone depend on the prayer of another? I can only answer with the return question. 'Why should my love be powerless to help another?' "

It is a beautiful question, and I believe that our love is never powerless to help. Thinking is powerful, and prayer is highly focused thinking, and it can be offered for good, and, alas, it can also be used for evil. The stories told about practitioners of the dark arts hurting and even killing people by the power of thought are not figments of the imagination; such things happen. But if the power of darkness is strong, the power of light is even stronger. In the physical world, the laser is a demonstration of the power of light. Love is power, and loving prayer is one of the greatest powers in the world.

As I was typing this page, the mail was put on my desk, and one of the letters was from a woman who questioned the prayers which are answered with a *No*, or, what is almost worse, with a hollow, echoing silence. I have had a great many *Yes* answers to prayers, but I have also had a great many *Noes*, including a decade-plus of my life which seemed to be nothing but *Noes*. I don't have any cut-and-dried answers to this. If I did, I could probably make a fortune as a psychologist.

The Book of Job is a struggle to understand this question: Why do terrible things happen to good people? Is it their "fault"? Is it part of something so great that we cannot understand it, or even our tiny role in the great drama? I have a friend who is a brilliant singer, and yet one event after another has kept her career from flourishing. Why? I have no answers. Only an offer of hope, of a tiny little flickering light of hope that cannot be extinguished no matter how many *Noes* we receive.

We do not like it that our love is often powerless to help in the way that we would wish. Sometimes our prayers for curing are answered with a Yes, sometimes with a No, and in the end, death comes for all of us. As I write this, a close friend of my own age is dying in great pain, dying of cancer. My love is powerless to save her life. But it is able to enter her suffering, as Jesus entered the suffering of all human creatures. It is not powerless to be part of the journey we all must take, from this known life into the unknown life of resurrection.

If our calling is to be co-creators, isn't the healing of all the brokenness and sorrow of the world part of that co-creating? Do we sometimes help in this great vocation in our dying as well as in our living?

George MacDonald writes:

" 'O God,' I said, and that was all. But what are the prayers of the whole universe more than the expression of that one cry? . . . He who seeks the Father more than anything He can give is likely to have what he asks, for he is not likely to ask amiss."

O God!

Lord Jesus Christ have mercy on me becomes more and more my deepest prayer, and the form in which I couch my intercessory prayer, and the *me* is never myself alone, for I, like quanta, cannot live in isolation, but only in relation to all others, to the Other.

We live not within ourselves but within God. In God we live and move and have our being. This is indeed mystery, but one which Jesus illuminated for us when he told the disciples to remember him when they broke bread and when they drank wine. Re-member. Make anew these members. Can these dry bones live again?

From Luke's gospel:

> *He took bread, and gave thanks, and brake it, and gave unto them, saying, This is my body which is given for you: this do in remembrance of me. Likewise also the cup after supper, saying, This cup is the new testament in my blood, which is shed for you.*

In God we live and move and have our being. God within us that we may be part of God, God's beauty our beauty, that we may be God's beauty. This is not magic. It is part of the miracle of the total unity of the universe. Thomas Aquinas writes:

> "The eucharistic food, instead of being transformed into the one who takes it, transforms him unto itself. It follows that the proper effect of the Sacrament is to transform us so much into Christ, that we can truly say: 'I live, now not I, but Christ liveth in me.' "

This is as gloriously true for those who view Communion as no more than a memorial service as for those who believe in the "real presence" in the transformed bread and wine. Transformed? Not into the actual corporeal body and blood of the dead Jew, Jesus of Nazareth, but into the risen body of the living Christ.

Lord Jesus Christ have mercy on me. May I be you, and you be me. May I be myself and my dying friend. Myself and my living friend, living in the new life of the risen Christ. May Christ have mercy on me and be in me as I grieve for my friend, for my parents, lovers, acquaintances, strangers dying in famine and flood and drought, all of creation groaning in travail until the redemption of all things, until the coming of the kingdom.

I learn my lessons slowly, seldom once for all. Continually they have to be learned and relearned, not with solemnity, but with awe and laughter and joy.

Grandfather George again: "It is the heart that is not yet sure of its God that is afraid to laugh in his presence."

And William Temple: "It is a great mistake to think that God is only or chiefly interested in religion."

So I learn with laughter, sometimes rueful laughter, as the Spirit teaches me with a sense of humour I have not always appreciated. But the wind blows where it will, and the Spirit moves how and where and as the holy Wind chooses.

———◆◆◆———

I, like most people, tend to make specific demands of God, not thinking them all the way through. And making specific demands thoughtfully is not a bad idea, for if we think seriously about what we are demanding, we may find out that it is not, in fact, something we want to ask for. Or we discover perhaps, that we do not want to ask it as unequivocally as we thought we did. Or, we may end up wanting simply, in our cloud of unknowing, to turn it over to God.

But sometimes—too often—we don't stop to think.

Because of faulty depth perception I have taken more than my share of falls, crashing down steps I have not seen. I have finally convinced my husband that when we are on vacation, in strange terrain, it is wise for him to walk slightly ahead of me, with me following a step behind, like a good Middle Eastern wife. If I see him going up, I know that I must step up. If he goes down, I know that I must step down. Often his hand comes out to warn, to guide me. But before this pattern was established, before he was convinced of the wisdom of what might superfically be considered discourtesy, there were two vacations in a row in which I had bad falls, damaging my psyche as well as my body, and losing a week of our vacation with bruises and pulled muscles and a body outraged at such violence.

The following year our vacation was on a freighter which left from Brooklyn and went to the great ports of Philadelphia, Baltimore and Newport News, and was then to head out into the Carribean; we were to fly home after having traversed the Panama Canal. The first days of the trip were cold and rainy, but marvellously relaxing. There was nothing we had to do, nowhere we had to be. It was total release from dailiness. On the first warm, sunny day I was sitting in a deck chair, writing, minding my own business, when the first sign of a sudden squall made the little ship lurch violently and the deck chair, with me in it, was flung across the deck. I put out my arm to break the fall, and spent the rest of the trip with my arm in a cast.

I was very angry, and totally unamused when I seemed to hear gentle laughter, and the words, *"But you didn't fall!"*

The following winter I left New York for a week of lecturing, first at Mundelein, then at Wheaton, then on to the Episcopal Diocese of Idaho—a very ecumenical jaunt.

As I was being driven from Mundelein to Wheaton, I felt a tightening in my throat, a hoarseness in my voice. All the signs said that I was coming down with a heavy laryn-geal cold. "Please," I prayed, "I have eleven more lectures to give. Please, please don't let me get laryngitis."

That evening I was a guest of honor at a small dinner party at Harold and Luci Shaw's. I had a wonderful time despite the fact that I definitely did not feel well. I went to the Lorentzens for the night, asked for a glass of orange juice for my throat, and went to bed, with apologies. The next day I felt miserable, but managed to get through the various assignments on my schedule.

That night I had to cut short my evening lecture. I was, fortunately, close to the end, when I realized that if I did not sit down I was going to faint. And when I wound down, rapidly, and sat down, I realized that I had to get to the bathroom, quickly. There was no way I was going to be able to attend the evening reception which had been planned to follow the lecture. I was driven back to the Lorentzens where I spent an exhausting night, rushing to the bathroom every few minutes. By morning I was expelling burning hot, clear fluid. It was, in fact, the worst attack of intestinal flu I had ever had.

But my voice was fine.

I was anything but amused by this turn of events. I said to myself, "If I was at home I'd go to bed for a week, and instead I have to go to Idaho."

I managed to give the Wheaton College chapel talk in the morning. Then Luci and two of my other friends drove me to O'Hare airport, broke all rules and carried my bags, and almost carried me, onto the plane where they prayed for me, with the laying on of hands. I'd never have made it otherwise. And only their sustaining prayers and amazing grace got me to Salt Lake City, where I had to change planes, and on to Idaho.

How should I have prayed? Are we never to ask for

specifics? Of course we are. That is how we find out whether or not our prayers are appropriate. We may always begin our prayers like the small child with the Christmas list. Only after we have gone through the "gimme" prayers can we let them go and move on to true prayer.

Jesus asked for specifics. In the Garden of Gethsemane he begged, with anguish, to be spared the horror of crucifixion. According to Mark:

> *My soul is exceeding sorrowful until death: tarry here, and watch. And he went forward a little, and fell on the ground, and prayed that, if it were possible, the hour might pass from him. And he said, Abba, Father, all things are possible with you; take away this cup from me: nevertheless not what I will, but what you will.*

And St. Luke adds:

> *And there appeared an angel from heaven, strengthening him.*

Yet, despite the comfort of the angel,

> *being in an agony he prayed more earnestly; and his sweat was as it were great drops of blood falling down to the ground.*

What is true of the great things is also true of the little things (are galaxies larger than quanta?). It is all right for us to pray for the continuing, full quality of life for those we love when they are ill. Sometimes it is given; sometimes it is not.

It is more than all right for my friends to continue to pray for my eyesight, and I accept this miracle with untellable joy, knowing also that at some time in the near or distant future this exterior vision may be taken from me. It is all right for me to pray for the small, silly things—Do not let me fall, Do not let me get laryngitis—as long as I hand the prayer, no matter how minor, no matter how foolish, to God. Your way, Lord, not mine.

Does Satan interfere in our prayer? Tempt us to plea-bargain, to try to manipulate? Or, more frightening, does he work for bodily death, for blindness, for self-centeredness? Probably. Satan does have tremendous power in this world. I cannot contradict Scripture. But his power is only temporal; it is not eternal. It may slow down the coming of the kingdom, but it cannot prevent its ultimate arrival. He may cause cancer and fire and obscenity and terrorism, but he cannot do so beyond a point. Love is always greater than hate, has more power than hate. The name of Jesus does make Satan shudder. The cross has the power of life over death. God's mercy is stronger than Satan's vindictiveness.

I doubt if I will ever unravel the mystery of intercessory prayer, for myself, for others. I know that there are powers of healing that Jesus tried to teach the disciples, and us, to tap. But the disciples could not throw out the unclean spirit from the possessed boy because their faith was not sufficient. If we had faith, we could indeed move mountains. And I learn faith, I deepen my faith, not only by exercising it but by reading Scripture, and contemplating the mighty acts of God. And perhaps most of all by being near people of faith, for faith is beautifully contagious.

I know that God does not want us to be ill, that el wants us to be whole. But sometimes our prayers for the cure of an illness belong to a transient, rather than an eternal whole-ness. We are trapped in the now and cannot see the eternal picture. For God's good reason, Paul's "thorn in the flesh," which he begged the Lord to take away, was of more use in God's purposes than would have been his curing. I do not know why my friend is dying young, and in pain; but my faith is nothing if I do not believe that in kairos, in God's time, she will be made whole, and that even now she can be used by God—as, indeed, she has been, during this illness, as a witness to gallantry, laughter, and joy. But ultimately God's will for her is wholeness, and I do not have to know how or when or where God's purpose for her, and for us, will be achieved.

Sometimes when I have not understood why God has not answered my prayer *my* way, it has been made clear to me later. Sometimes when it has seemed that my way has been done, I have learned later that it was not the best way. I am gradually learning to turn everything over to God, sometimes grudgingly, often argumentatively (like my favourite Old Testament characters), but I am still learning.

A Fountain
in the
Desert
11

WE TEND TO SKIP over or disparage parts of Scripture, such as Abraham's passing Sarah off as his sister, or Lot's daughters sleeping with their father, because such distasteful events arose out of cultures vastly different from our own. We have damaged each other and ourselves in the name of Christ in our contempt for and ill-treatment of Indians and Africans and Asians; because they, too, have cultures different from our own, we are suspicious of them. Like the people of Sodom, who called Lot a foreigner, we assume that because foreigners are not "us" they are therefore not as good as we are.

F. S. C. Northrup in *The Meeting of East and West* writes:

Nothing is more evil and tragically devastating in actual consequence than one's own moral and religious ideals, fine as they may be, when they are accompanied by ignorance and resultant provincialism and blindness with respect to people and cultures different from one's own.

A careful and steady reading of Scripture helps free us from this insularism. Jesus spoke and ate not only with sinners, but with foreigners; with "them"—with Samaritans, who were looked down on with contempt by the good, middle-class people of his day; with a Syro-Phoenician woman; with the Roman enemy. He made it clear that people who are different are not therefore inferior. He knocked all our race and class distinctions to smithereens.

So. Lot and his daughters were saved from the destruction of Sodom and Gomorrah, and Abraham moved from Mamre to Gerar, and once again tried to pass Sarah off as his sister, this time to King Abimelech. But God warned the king in a dream not to touch her. Abimelech heeded the dream, and was, to put it mildly, annoyed at Abraham for his deception. Then,

> *The Lord blessed Sarah, as he had promised, and she became pregnant, and bore a son to Abraham when he was old.*

With man such a thing is impossible. With God nothing is impossible. Sarah's prayers were answered, not in human time, but in God's time.

> *The boy was born at the time when God said he would be born. Abraham named him Isaac, and when Isaac was eight days old Abraham circumcised him... Abraham was a hundred years old when Isaac was born. Sarah said, "God has brought me joy and laughter."*

Now she could acknowledge her laughter, could revel in it and share it and rejoice in it. She said,

> *"Everyone who hears about it will laugh with me...*
> *Who would have said to Abraham that Sarah would*
> *nurse children? Yet I have borne him a son in his old*
> *age."*

I think often about Sarah's prayer, answered not in human time, but in God's time. In a way, the very outrageousness of the time in which Sarah conceived and gave birth is a re-emphasis of the truth that God is not restricted by time;

> *The child grew, and on the day that he was weaned,*
> *Abraham gave a great feast.*

How fathers love to give parties for their children! We can almost think of those first mighty acts of creation as the grandest party ever thrown, and ever since, God has thrown a party whenever possible.

And of course, as with anything good, Satan and the fallen creatures he has gathered around him, angelic and human, move in and distort the good, so we get the excesses of cocktail parties and sex orgies, parties which are not parties at all in the real sense of the word. How lovely real parties are! Every time one of the children has been away and comes home we have a party, candles on the table, and flowers, and maybe presents, and meals cooked with loving care, even if it's mostly vegetables from the garden. A party is a celebration of love, just as a punishment is a lesson of love.

———◆◆◆———

One day Sarah saw Isaac playing with Ishmael, the son of Hagar—Hagar who had scorned Sarah's barrenness—

Laughter playing with Bitterness. And Sarah still had bitterness over Hagar's scorn lodged like a splinter of ice deep in her heart; and when she saw the two boys playing together she was afraid.

So she went to Abraham and asked him to send Hagar and Ishmael away, so that Ishmael would not inherit anything that Sarah felt belonged rightfully to Isaac.

Abraham was troubled. Ishmael was his son, too. But God informed him that it was all right to do what Sarah had asked; el would take care of Ishmael. So Abraham gave Hagar

> *some food and a leather bag full of water. He put the child on her back and sent her away. She left and wandered about in the wilderness of Beersheba. When the water was all gone she left the child under a bush and ... said, "I can't bear to see my child die." And she began to cry.*

So did her son.

> *God heard the boy crying, and from heaven the angel of the Lord spoke to Hagar: "What are you troubled about, Hagar? Don't be afraid."*

Don't be afraid! How often the Lord's angels start their conversations with us this way: Don't be afraid! Don't be afraid, the angel Gabriel said to Zacharias and later to the fourteen-year-old Mary. Don't be afraid, an angel told the shepherds on the hill outside Bethlehem.

We need this reassurance. Even for those of us who believe implicitly in angels, to be confronted by one is an awesome thing.

So the angel reassured Hagar and continued,

"God has heard the boy crying. Get up, go and pick him up, and comfort him. I will make a great nation out of his descendants." Then God opened Hagar's eyes, and she saw a well

where no well had been before. "Why are you troubled? Don't be afraid," God's angel reminds us over and over again. "Let not your heart be troubled. You believe in me. It will be all right," Jesus told his anxious friends. *What* will be all right? If I put my arms around you and comfort you and say, "Let not your heart be troubled, it will be all right," what am I promising?

In the world's terms, nothing. In the world's terms I am being a lie and a cheat to give such empty comfort. There are miracles, indubitably. But there are other times when the answer is No, or silence. When we put our arms around someone to give comfort, we cannot bring the dead back to life, or keep the spouse from walking out in favour of someone else, or stop the course of debilitating illness. We cannot prevent flood or drought or war. So what does the promise that "it will be all right" mean? *What* will be all right?

God's purpose. God's purpose for us and for all of creation. In God's time. In kairos. El did not prevent Abraham from sending Hagar and Ishmael into the wilderness. And Hagar had no way of knowing that many generations later, when Joseph's brothers would sell him to some merchants, those same merchants would be descendants of Ishmael.

God's purpose. God's plan. The Great Dance, the ancient harmonies, weaving and interweaving to make the pattern perfect. Often it is difficult to see that there is any pattern. We are too small to see the richness of the whole.

But all of creation is pattern, from the Great Dance of the galaxies to the equally Great Dance of the submicroscopic, subatomic particles, existing only because they are dancing together. Satan tried to make dissonances, to interrupt the rhythm, to distort the pattern. One of his most successful ploys is to make us believe that his distortions of the original good have destroyed that good. But they have not. It is only the distortions we must fear and shun, never the original good itself, kything, singing and dancing, loving.

God created, and saw that it was good. In the beginning was the Word, the Word which is the Light that the darkness can neither snuff out nor comprehend.

The Lord told Abraham that it was all right to give in to Sarah's fears and emotional wounds and send Hagar and Ishmael away, and then this God of creation produced a well where there had been no well before. The skeptic might say, "The well was underground all the time and just happened to break surface at that moment." But did not God *choose* to have the waters break surface at that moment? As he chose to allow the waters of the Red Sea to divide at the particular moment in which Moses needed to lead his people out of Egypt? If all of Creation belongs to God because el made it, el can do what el wills with it, and what el wills may, to us, be miracle.

But we never earn or deserve our miracles. Often the most deserving people don't get them. God always hears our cries, but sometimes el does not answer in a way we think fair, and because we are too small to see the whole pattern, we don't understand why. And not all the No answers come from God. Illness and accident and death can come from man in his fallenness, from the temporary victories of the enemy.

More people have been killed in automobile accidents than in all of the wars in all of our history. And surely those who invented the internal combustion engine and made cars and airplanes had no idea that it was going to cost so heavily in human life. It was an example of what we know with our intellects being far ahead of our wisdom to understand all the implications.

It was the desire to *know* which led us to explore the heart of the atom. The desire to know is part of what makes us human, and in its proper rhythm it is a creative desire. But, alas, it was the Second World War which accelerated the interest in splitting the atom and provided the enormous funds needed for research, which would not have been available in peace time: the rhythm distorted again. Surely if those first atomic scientists in New Mexico had had the slightest idea where their experiments were going to lead, if time had curved and they had seen visions of the victims of Hiroshima or Nagasaki, they might well not have exploded that first atom bomb.

But what we already know, we know. That's one of the messages implicit in the story of Adam and Eve. We cannot turn our backs on what we know, or bury our heads in the sand. We need to try to find wisdom enough so that our knowledge will serve us and the rest of the human race creatively and not destructively.

How, O Lord, do we learn wisdom as well as knowledge? It is somewhat like miracle and magic. Wisdom, like miracle, is yours, Lord, and to be received as gift. The enemy tries to keep us from it, by praising us for our great knowledge, *our* knowledge, and so shattering us into further fragments. But the Spirit who danced upon the face of the waters in the beginning and who came to us as Comforter after the Ascension will help to heal us, will help to mend our broken pieces with spiritual glue so that the break does not even show.

God can and does come into the most terrible things and

redeem them. I do not believe that God wills cancer, or multiple sclerosis. I do not believe that we are ever to regard the brutal death of a child as God's will. I know only that el can come into whatever happens, and by being part of it, can return it to wholeness. This is a large part of the meaning of incarnation. Nothing ever happens to us alone. It happens to God, too.

This used to be considered heresy, but yesterday's heresy is today's truth. Within our own century it was taught in seminary that God is impassible, that he is inaccessible to injury, and therefore does not and cannot suffer. What does such teaching make of the Suffering Servant passages in Isaiah? What does it do to the Incarnation? To the Cross? If Jesus was fully man as well as fully God, surely he suffered. This impassibility of God makes no sense to me. If Jesus suffered, but God did not, what does that do to the concept of the Trinity, except split it into polytheism? The impassibility of God seems totally incompatible with everything I read in the Bible, and with all my experience.

God cared about Ishmael, crying with terror there in the wilderness.

God cares about us, for our Lord is in us and we are in our Lord, and el's beauty is our beauty and all of creation is an act of creative love.

Towards the end of her book, *Peter Abelard*, Helen Waddell writes:

> "My God," said Thibault, "what's that?"
>
> From somewhere near them in the woods a cry had risen, a thin cry, of such intolerable anguish that Abelard turned dizzy on his feet, and caught at the wall.
>
> "It's a child's voice," he said. "Oh, God, are they at a child?"
>
> Thibault had gone outside. The cry came again,

making the twilight and the firelit hearth a mockery.

"A rabbit," said Thibault. He listened... "It'll be in a trap... Christ!" The scream came yet again.

Abelard was beside him, and the two plunged down the bank.

"Down by the river," said Thibault. "I saw them playing, God help them, when I was coming home. You know the way they go demented with fun in the evenings. It will have been drumming with its hind paws to itself and brought down the trap."

Abelard went on, hardly listening. "Oh, God," he was muttering. "Let it die. Let it die quickly."

But the cry came yet again. On the right, this time. He plunged through a thicket of hornbeam.

"Watch out," said Thibault, thrusting past him. "The trap might take the hand off you."

The rabbit stopped shrieking when they stooped over it, either from exhaustion, or in some last extremity of fear. Thibault held the teeth of the trap apart, and Abelard gathered up the little creature in his hands. It lay for a moment breathing quickly, then in some blind recognition of the kindness that had met it at the last, the small head thrust and nestled against his arm, and it died.

It was this last confiding thrust that broke Abelard's heart. He looked down at the little draggled body, his mouth shaking. "Thibault," he said, "do you think there is a God at all? Whatever has come to me, I earned it. But what did this one do?"

Thibault nodded.

"I know," he said. "Only—I think God is in it too."

Abelard looked up sharply.

"In it? Do you mean that it makes Him suffer, the way it does us?"

Again Thibault nodded.

"Then why doesn't He stop it?"

"I don't know," said Thibault. "Unless—unless it's like the Prodigal Son. I suppose the father could have kept him at home against his will. But what would have been the use? All this," he stroked the limp body, "is because of us. But all the time God suffers. More than we do."

God is in it, too.

That was the great difference between the God of the nomadic Hebrew and the multiple gods of the other tribes. Abraham's and Sarah's God cared.

But when he told them to leave their comfortable home and go into an unknown country, he didn't coerce them. They obeyed because they chose to obey, not because God forced them. They could have been like the Prodigal Son, choosing the fleshpots. But they listened, and they obeyed, and they went into the unknown, and God was with them.

God is in it, whatever it is, with us.

That is heresy, Abelard and Thibault were taught, heresy still being taught in some seminaries. But God, in it, with us, is the only God I can believe in. It was the tempter who thought up impassibility and labelled as heresy the idea that God is part of all of creation, and suffers whenever any part of creation suffers. But what else does the Incarnation affirm? How else do we pray, except to the Maker of ourselves who loves us enough to be part of us? What else do we affirm when we do as Jesus taught us to do and take the bread and drink the wine and affirm that el's beauty is our beauty and that we are in el and el is in us and all, all, is el's?

So God heard Ishmael crying, as only a small, thirsty, frightened little boy can cry, and in the dry desert wilderness the Master of the Universe brought up a fountain of water.

The God
Who Cannot Fail
12

GOD BROKE OPEN a fountain in the dry, parched land of the desert in order to quench the thirst of a child. And after we read this evidence of God's loving concern for the lost little things of creation, we are taken back to the center of the story of Abraham and Sarah.

Everything is going pleasantly for them. Abraham makes a treaty with Abimelech, also about a well (wells are of crucial importance in any desert land) where Abraham plants a tamarisk tree and worships the living Lord.

It seemed that Abraham and Sarah in their old age had everything they wanted. And then God called, again:

> "Abraham!" And Abraham answered, "Yes, here I am!"
> "Take your son," God said, "your only son, Isaac, whom you love so much, and go to the land of Moriah.

There on a mountain that I will show you, offer him as a sacrifice to me."

There follows no cry of outrage or rebellion. Perhaps what God asked was beyond the bounds of outrage and rebellion. Other gods demanded human sacrifice, or displayed anger that could only be appeased by blood. But those were *other* gods, gods who didn't care about their people. The difference between the God of the Hebrews and the gods of the neighbouring tribes was that God does care about el's people. They matter.

So how could God ask such a thing of Abraham?

Christians have been criticized by other theists for equating the sacrifice of Abraham with the sacrifice of God the Father when his son was crucified. I don't think God ever tells the same story twice. One story can help us understand another; we know more about human confusion because of Hamlet than we would otherwise, but no other story is the story of Hamlet. From Oedipus we know more about the terrible fact that even an unwitting sin must be punished than we would otherwise, but no other story is the story of Oedipus. The great drama of Jesus of Nazareth is unique, independent of the complex drama of Abraham and Sarah and their son. We may see a pattern that links them, but to equate the two is to show a misunderstanding of the Trinity.

The story of God's terrible demand of Abraham is unique and has unique things to tell us. How could a loving Lord, a Lord who cares about el's creatures, for whom the tiniest atom is of the utmost importance, the hair on a head, the fate of a sparrow, how could the Master of the Universe ask such an unnatural, impossible thing of Abraham?

How indeed? The question has haunted us for several thousand years. In the Middle Ages, God's demand of Abraham was often the subject of miracle and morality plays. In the beginning of *Fear and Trembling* Kierkegaard retells the story of Abraham and Isaac three different ways and still he reaches no conclusion; even today we cannot understand it unless God reveals its meaning to us. Our only proper response is silence, a silence that is echoed following the words from the cross, "My God, my God, why hast thou forsaken me?"

In Jerusalem, inside the old city, I went to the great gold mosque which the devout Jew cannot enter because the mosque is built over the place where the temple stood and no one knows exactly where the Holy of Holies was placed. The Holy of Holies is so sacred that the place where it stood so long ago may not be stepped on, even inadvertantly. I went in, with my shoes off, feeling deep awe (Moses took his shoes off before the burning bush, and so must we when we approach God's holy places), and I stood in front of a great spreading rock, the rock where Abraham laid Isaac and raised his knife to kill his son, and my skin prickled. In my bare feet I stood there, lost in wonder at the magnificent incomprehensibility of the Creator, who loves us so much that he came to live with us and be part of us and die for us and rise again for us and send the Holy Spirit to comfort us. And I was, somehow, comforted by the very incomprehensibility of all that makes life creative and worth living.

The story continues:

> *Early the next morning Abraham cut some wood for the sacrifice, loaded his donkey, and took Isaac and two servants with him.*

How must Sarah have felt? What kind of laughter was there in this? Did Abraham tell her what God had asked of him, tell her perhaps at the last moment in order to avoid her tears and protestations? Or did he just take the boy and go? Scripture says nothing, but Sarah was a mother. She had known Abraham for a long time, and there was no way he could have hidden from her the heaviness of his heart.

So perhaps she got it out of him. "Abraham, something's wrong. What is it? Tell me." And then perhaps he unburdened himself. It is not good for the human creature to be alone. And what a burden that was for Abraham to carry, much heavier than for the boy. He must have told Sarah, his helpmeet.

In my ears across the centuries I can hear the echo of Sarah's cry. "God! You know nothing about being a mother!"

Our perception of God has grown and changed through the centuries, but we still have learned little about the mother in the godhead, we have focused so consistently on the father. I understand Sarah's cry, and the medieval mystics' radiant affirmation of Christ as sister, lover, All in all. We need that intuitive and casual knowing that as God is in all things, el is also in both sexes; the brittle insistence on God's femaleness is as limited as the old paternalism.

But Sarah knew about being a mother and, after all she had been through, I doubt if she would have hesitated to tell God where el was lacking.

Abraham started out for the place that God had told him about. On the third day he saw the place in the distance. He said to his men, "Stay here with the donkey while the boy and I go over there; and when we have worshipped we will come back to you."

So Abraham took the wood for the sacrifice and laid it on Isaac's shoulder; he himself carried the fire and the knife, and the two of them went on together.

Isaac said to Abraham, "Father!"

And he answered, "What is it, my son?"

Isaac said, "Here are the fire and the wood, but where is the lamb for the sacrifice?"

Abraham answered, "God himself will provide a lamb for the sacrifice, my son." And the two of them went on together to the place of which God had spoken.

There Abraham built an altar and arranged the wood. He bound his son Isaac and laid him on the altar on top of the wood.

What spareness in the telling of the story! Not an extraneous detail. Here I am quoting largely from the *New English Bible*, but in all the translations I have checked there is the same simplicity, the same control, enough to keep us wondering for centuries. Did Isaac realize what was happening? Did he scream with terror? Did he beg to be released? Did he try to resist, to escape, to run away? Abraham

took the knife to kill his son; but the angel of the Lord called to him from heaven, "Abraham! Abraham!"

He answered, "Here I am."

The angel of the Lord said, "Do not raise your hand against the boy. Do not touch him. Now I know that you have obedient reverence for God, because you have not withheld from me your son, your only son."

You have not withheld from *me*. The angel is speaking in the voice of the Lord, elself.

Abraham looked up, and there he saw a ram caught by its horns in a thicket. So he went and took the ram and offered it as a sacrifice instead of his son. Abraham named the place Jehovah-jireh; and to this day the saying is: "In the mountain of the Lord it was provided."

> *Then the angel of the Lord called from heaven a second time to Abraham, "This is the word of the Lord: by my own self I swear: because you have done this, and have not withheld your son, your only son, I will bless you abundantly and greatly multiply your descendants until they are as numerous as the stars in the sky and the grains of sand on the sea shore."*

Perhaps this story tells us more about the nature of man's understanding of God than it does about God elself. The story is staggering in its simplicity. It never falters. Its very straightforwardness, its lack of explanation is one of the most difficult things about it.

But the Bible is for me—I repeat—the living Word of God, although I do not need to believe that it was divinely dictated by God in a long beard and white gown (a picture of Moses, again) and written down in a moment of time by an angel scribe. It is a great story book written over a great many centuries by many people. And when I call it a great story I am emphasizing that it is a great book of Truth. It is the truth by which I live. I do not understand it all, but that does not make it any less the truth.

During the writing of this I was asked to tell, during an interview for a Christian magazine, what Jesus meant in my life. I think I know what I was supposed to say, but though most of the things I was supposed to say are true, they don't sound natural to me; they sound out of context with the God who created everything and everybody and called it all good. So I answered that Jesus taught me about story, the truth of story, and that story is light.

Sometimes the light of the story seems veiled or shadowed, no matter how we struggle to seek for its meaning.

After his terrible experience, we may ask ourselves—

could Isaac ever have trusted his father again? Was Abraham's response to God changed? What are we to understand? How does God's demand of Abraham fit in with el's love for all creation? Was Isaac's fear of as much consequence to God as Ishmael's tears?

I am still waiting for the telephone call which will tell me that my college friend is dead, and I know that even though those of us who love her deeply may not be near her hospital bed, we are nevertheless with her. And I think of a mutual friend who died a few years ago at ninety-three, a great lady of vision and laughter who never lost her ability to change and to go into the unknown, and I feel that she is waiting at the gates, to hold out her hand and say, "See! El has not forgotten you; you are carved in the palm of his hand. As am I, and all of creation. See! You can be with and pray for those you love even better here than you could before! See! El has created you to *be,* and it is good."

Today the great blue spruce which we planted as a tiny seedling, far, far from the house at Crosswicks, had to be cut down. In thirty years the little plant had grown into an enormous tree which not only shaded us from the glare of the hot, setting sun in summer, but whose roots were beginning to undermine the old foundations of the house. It is the spruce our son once used for a ladder when he came home from a late night swim with friends and did not want to disturb his sleeping grandmother. Now there is a great new space of air where the spruce stood; it seems the atoms have not yet gathered together within its outline.

And it is somehow all part of the story. Perhaps one day that rock I saw in the mosque in Jerusalem will be gone, that rock on which Abraham bound and laid Isaac, but the story will not be gone. And I do not have to understand, not Isaac's ultimate death, after Jacob had cheated Esau out of the blessing which should have been his; not the cutting down of the great spruce (it's only a tree, they said), not even my own lack of understanding.

In his second letter to the Corinthians, Paul writes (and now I am turning to the *Jerusalem Bible*):

He has said, "My grace is enough for you; my power is at its best in weakness." So [says Paul] I shall be very happy to make my weaknesses my special boast so that the power of Christ may stay over me.

And that, too, is what Christ means to me, that God can come to me in my weakness and poverty and still find use for it and say that this, too, is good, is very good.

In *Messengers of God*, Elie Wiesel writes:

And Abraham sacrificed the ram in place of his son.

Poor ram, said certain sages. God tests man and the ram is killed. That is unjust; after all, he has done nothing.

Said Rabbi Yehoshua: This ram had been living in Paradise since the sixth day of creation, waiting to be called. He was destined from the very beginning to replace Isaac on the altar.

A special ram, with a unique destiny, of whom Rabbi Hanina ben Doss said: Nothing of the sacrifice was lost. The ashes were dispersed in the Temple's sanctuary; the sinews David used as chords for his harp; the skin was claimed by the prophet Elijah to clothe himself; as for the horns, the smaller one called the people together at the foot of Mount Sinai and the larger one will resound one day, announcing the coming [the first? or the second?] of the Messiah.

Again we confront the problem of free will. Did the ram have to come, to play his part in the drama, to get his horns caught in the bushes, and to be killed in place of Isaac? Did he not have a choice to say yes, or to say no?

In the parable of the two sons, when the father asked them to go work in the vineyard for him, the elder said, "Of course, Father, I will," and did not go. The younger son said, "I won't," and then thought better of it and went.

There is also a legend that Mary was not the first young woman to whom the angel came. But she was the first one to say yes.

And how unsurprising it would be for a fourteen-year-old girl to refuse the angel. To be disbelieving. Or to say:

> *"Are you sure you mean—*
> *but I'm unworthy—*
> *I couldn't, anyhow—*
> *I'd be afraid. No, no,*
> *it's inconceivable, you can't be asking me—*
> *I know it's a great honour*
> *but wouldn't it upset them all,*
> *both our families?*
> *They're very proper, you see.*
> *Do I have to answer now?*
> *I don't want to say no—*
> *it's what every girl hopes for*
> *even if she won't admit it.*
> *But I can't commit myself to anything*
> *this important without turning it over*
> *in my mind for a while*
> *and I should ask my parents*
> *and I should ask my—*
> *Let me have a few days to think it over."*

Sorrowfully, although he was not surprised
to have it happen again,
the angel returned to heaven.

Who could not understand such hesitation in a young woman—fear of the whole wild thing being misunderstood, fear that she would be considered an adulteress (for any woman taken in adultery was stoned to death)?

God will never force us. If we are to be co-creators with el, we must be co-creators willingly. Or maybe that's wrong. Unlike Mary, not all the prophets were immediately willing. They were often like the younger son who said, "I won't" but ended up doing what God had asked. Even if they had to spend three days in the belly of a great fish before they thought better of the Lord's request and went off grudgingly to preach repentance—whether they, personally, wanted the people to repent and be saved, or not.

So perhaps we need not be immediately willing. We can argue and protest that it's too difficult, that we aren't up to it, that we deserve a little rest for a change, that dying by stoning is a nasty way to die. And then we can say, still a bit grudgingly, "Here I am. Send me. Be it unto me according to your word." And then we will be given the strength to do whatever it is that God wants us to do, to bear whatever it is that God wants us to bear. If God wants us to bear figs out of season, el, the Creator, will give us the ability to do so.

Long before I read Wiesel's words, I had been thinking a good deal about the ram, as well as the human characters I was reading and thinking about. To help me think, I have, throughout the years, written poems in the voices of some of the characters in the stories in Scripture, in order to understand better what they have to say to me, that I may move from reading to thinking to prayer.

Here is one from the point of view of the ram.

THE GOD WHO CANNOT FAIL

Caught in the Bush

Asked to leave Eden
where I, with all the other beasts,
remained after the two human creatures left,
I moved to the gates.
The cherub with the flaming sword
drew aside to let me by,
folding his wings across his eyes.

I trotted along a path which led through woods,
across a desert, made a long detour
around a lake, and finally climbed a mountain
till trees gave way to bushes
and a rock.
An old man raised a knife.
He stood there by the rock
and wept and raised his knife.
So these are men, I thought,
and shook my head in horror, and was caught
within the springing branches of a bush.
Then there was lightning, and the thunder came,
and a voice cried out to me: My son, my son,
slain before the foundation of the world.

And then I felt the knife.
For this I came from Eden;
my will is ever his,
as I am his, and have my life
in him, and he in me.

Thus the knife pierced his own heart,
in piercing mine,
and the old man laughed for joy.

If God created everything, and saw that it was good, then we have much to learn from all that good, from the ram, from the robins who had the courage and the hope to build their nest outdoors in the trees this spring, to my old Irish setter, needing to be close either to the other dogs or to one of us, needing the assurance of touch. The other animals, instead of shunning him as old age leads him towards death, provide him with their own equivalent of handholding: Titus, the amber cat, continues his old job of cleaning Timothy's ears, putting one paw firmly on the old setter's head as he cleans and licks, as though the big beast were the size of a kitten. Tiyē, the Ibezan hound puppy, a beautiful, galloping reproduction of the temple dogs in Egyptian friezes, licks the old dog's watery eyes. And this concern is part of the good which we human beings have lost, and are at last beginning to recognize that we have lost; and so there is hope that it may once again be recovered.

The telephone call that I have been waiting for, these last several weeks, has come at last. But before it came, my friend and I said our good-byes, and somehow the telephone was not between us. In the truest sense of the word we kythed, and I was able to tell her of the dream I had of her and our ninety-three-year-old friend, the two of them dancing together in a field of daisies, dancing in the joy that is part of the dance of all creation.

"Oh, how beautiful, how beautiful," she said.

And we kythed our love and hope.

And at the same time I was cooking and cleaning and preparing for a houseparty to celebrate the double fiftieth birthday of two of our friends, with the attic once more turned into a dormitory, and the kitchen smelling of homemade pasta. And it is all part of the mighty act of creation and it is good.

We can recognize the holy good even while we are achingly, fearfully aware of all that has been done to it through greed and lust for power and blind stupidity. We forget the original good of all creation because of our own destructiveness. The ugly fact that evil can be willed for people by other people, and that the evil comes to pass, does not take away our capacity to will good. There may be many spirits abroad other than the Holy Spirit (the Gospels warn us of them), but they do not make the Holy Spirit less holy. Our paradoxes and contradictions expand; our openness to God's revelations to us must also be capable of expansion. Our religion must always be subject to change without notice—our religion, not our faith, but the patterns in which we understand and express our faith. Surely we would feel ill at ease today with people who had family morning prayers and Scripture readings daily, and yet kept slaves?

Our perception of faith in our Creator is of necessity different from Abraham's and Sarah's perception—neither better nor worse, but different. But since all, all, is part of God, then the differences are part of el, too, for el is All in all, and is loving us tenderly in order to redeem all that was made in the beginning, so that it may once again be called very good.

And I am convinced that not only is our planet ultimately to be freed from bondage to Satan, but with it the whole universe—all the singing, dancing suns and stars and galaxies—will one day join unhindered in the great and joyous festival. The glorious triumph of Easter will encompass the whole of God's handiwork. The praise for the primal goodness of God's creation in the beginning will be rounded out with the final worship, as John has expressed it in the Revelation:

"Worthy art thou, our Lord and God, to receive glory and honour and power, for thou didst create all things, and by thy will they existed and were created." And I heard every creature in heaven and on earth and under the earth and in the sea, and all therein, saying, "To him who sits upon the throne and to the Lamb be blessing and honour and glory and might for ever and ever. Amen!"

———◆◆◆———

I look at the colours of autumn moving across the land, and even now creation is ablaze with glory. The oak trees are touched with purply-bronze. The maples flame scarlet and gold. We are harvesting vegetables from the garden, grateful that an early frost has not touched the delicate green peppers, the sweet corn, the tomatoes; or the zinnias and marigolds which border the garden and protect it from Japanese beetles. We have startled an enterprising rabbit sitting in the middle of the greenery, eating lettuce and green beans, bold as brass as long as the dogs are indoors.

Sometimes at dusk we see the loveliness of a doe and her fawn walking across the field, but they have stayed away from the garden, chewing instead the bark of tender new trees.

Broccoli, Brussels sprouts, carrots, don't mind the cold. We'll be picking them long after the ground is rimed with frost. We have discovered a new vegetable this summer, spaghetti squash, which we scrape out with a fork, after cooking, in long, spaghetti-like strands. Leeks are a delight, creamed, or in soup, and spinach salad. We glory in the goodness of creation every day. All that weed-pulling was worth it, though weeds have their own beauty, and, like mosquitoes and flies, are an inevitable part of the summer.

At night now the sky is clear, with no heat haze. One

night we eat supper out on the little terrace which we have made with flagstones and lots of honest sweat. We linger at the picnic table through sunset and star rise, and suddenly someone says, "How light it is on the northern horizon!" We blow out the lamps and there is the staggering beauty of the Northern Lights. There is something primal about those lights pulsing, in pale green and rose, upwards from the horizon. They give me the same surge of joy as the unpolluted horizon near the Strait of Magellan, showing the curve of the home planet; the same lifting of the heart as the exuberance of the dolphins sporting about the ship after we had crossed the equator.

I sit at the table as we all watch the awesome display of beauty, and there again is the promise of the rainbow covenant which God placed in the sky; and there, too, is the fulfilled new covenant of Easter, radiant, affirming.

And it is good.

In those northern lights, in the great river of the Milky Way, in the circle of family and friends around the table, and in the meal we have just finished and which came largely from the garden, I see God, and the joy we have jointly with him in creation.

In his first letter, John writes,

My dear people, we are already the children of God, but what we are to be in the future has not yet been revealed; all we know is, that when it is revealed we shall be like him, because we shall see him as he really is.

Not only do all our human hopes and dreams look forward to that time of reunion with God. Paul, writing to the Romans, tells us that

The whole creation waits with eager longing for the revealing of the sons of God. The creation itself will be set

free from its bondage to decay, and obtain the glorious
liberty of God's children... We know that the whole
creation has been groaning in travail together until now.

In writing to the people of Colossae, Paul goes even further
in his hope for the future:

For in Christ all the fulness of God was pleased to dwell
and through him to reconcile himself to all things,
whether on earth or in heaven.

We, on our small planet, can either help with this cosmic
reconciliation, or we can hinder it. Hardness of heart
hinders the coming of the kingdom. Smugness, pride, self
absorption, hinders it. "You are a stiff-necked people,"
God chided the children of Israel, and we are still a stiff-
necked people and that, too, hinders the coming of the kingdom.

But if I believe that God is not going to fail with me, I
must also believe, with Paul and John, that el is not going to
fail with anybody, or Satan has won. El will not fail with the
gypsy moth caterpillar nor the encephalitis mosquito nor
the rapist nor the war monger nor any part of all that el has
made for his own delight—and ours, too. El will not fail,
otherwise el is allowing Satan to keep this planet forever. I
do not believe that this can happen, for we are God's, and it
is el who has made us and not we ourselves.

And as long as I have even a small splinter of unloving-
ness lodged in my heart, how can I look down on or judge
anybody else? Jesus says that I must not. I know that I cannot throw the first stone, and I hope that, no matter how
many sinful prodigal sons are invited, I will still want to go to
the party.

If I believe in the loving Abba to whom Jesus prayed, then I must also believe that this loving father is not going to fail with creation, that the glorious triumph of Easter will ultimately be extended to the entire universe.

Namasté

In the beginning God created the heaven and the earth.
In the beginning was the Word, and the Word was with
God, and the Word was God.
And the Spirit moved upon the face of the waters.
And God saw that it was good. It was very good.

At sea, on the S. S. Santa Mariana, 1981,
to Crosswicks, autumn, 1982